Published by Jerry Savelle Ministries
Crowley, Texas, U.S.A.
www.jerrysavelle.org
Printed in the U.S.A.

ISBN 978-1-939934-04-8

Rights for publishing this book outside the U.S.A. or in non-English languages are
administered by Jerry Savelle Ministries, an international not-for-profit ministry. For
additional information, please visit jerrysavelle.org or, email info@jsmi.org, or write to
Jerry Savelle Ministries, PO Box 748, Crowley, TX 76036, U.S.A.

To order copies of this book and other resources in bulk quantities,
please contact us at 1-817-297-3155.

THE SPIRIT OF
FAVOR
ON YOUR
HOUSE

JERRY SAVELLE

CONTENTS

Introduction

For those of us who live in Texas, the arrival of spring is traditionally marked by two things. One is the bursting forth of the Texas bluebonnets. Considered by many to be the state's most beautiful wildflowers, these colorful bloomers create a blanket of blue that covers the rolling prairies and roadsides of Texas. But the brilliant beauty of the bluebonnets is often overshadowed by ominous dark skies and the ever-present threat of tornadoes.

Over a period of three days in May, 2013, an outbreak of some sixteen tornadoes struck parts of northern and eastern Texas, including Granbury, a historic lake community located about thirty-five miles from Fort Worth. Carolyn and I have owned a lake house there for more than thirty years, so when I heard about the first storms, I drove down there to check on it.

I was relieved to find no damage in our neighborhood, so I went inside the house and decided to call and check on a friend of mine who also lived in the area. As I was looking out the window at the lake,

I watched as a tornado began to form, its vortex extending downward toward the lake right in front of me. I immediately started rebuking that thing, and it quickly ascended. As I stood praying, it came down and went back up two more times before remaining grounded as it headed straight for my house.

All of a sudden I felt the walls begin to shake, and I heard the sound of wood snapping. I moved to the safety of the hallway to avoid any flying glass, all the while proclaiming, "God's blessing is upon this house! God's favor is upon this house!"

That crazy thing came right up to my property. For a while, it was so dark and windy outside that I couldn't see a thing. I thought that funnel was going to suck the roof right off of the house, but just as quickly as it came, the tornado left. When I went outside to survey the damage, I saw some of the trees on our property had been downed. The largest tree was now lying squarely across the deck, but the deck was not damaged. That tornado took down some trees, but it didn't break one board on the deck, and not one shingle was missing from my roof.

Sometime later my wife, Carolyn, and I went to the local landscape nursery to purchase new trees to replace those we'd lost. Until that day, I hadn't realized what it cost to replace large trees. The woman who checked us out gave us a generous discount, and she said she'd even arrange to have the trees delivered free of charge. I looked at Carolyn and said, "That's the favor of God!"

The favor of God not only had protected our house, but it also allowed us to have the world's very best new trees without having to pay the world's price for them.

These occurrences were not mere coincidences. When something like this happens only once, it may be a coincidence. But when it happens every day of your life—as it does in mine—it can only be explained as the *favor of God* in operation.

What God does for me on a regular basis, He also wants to do for you. He is no respecter of persons. The only difference between what God does for me and what happens (or doesn't happen) in the lives of others is this: For some, "the favor of God" is a nice sermon title. For me, operating in the favor of God is a lifestyle.

Many years ago, when I found out I could have God's blessing and favor upon my house, I started decreeing it my life and leaning heavily upon it. This lifestyle I've chosen has opened the door to the miraculous in my life.

In 1997, I wrote a book entitled *Walking in Divine Favor*. That book was sold literally around the world, introducing scores of people to the biblical truths concerning the favor of God. By 2012, God had given me a considerable amount of new revelation about His favor and how it operates. So I wrote a new book that included all of the material from *Walking in Divine Favor* and several other publications, as well as the more recent revelation on the topic. That book, entitled (not surprisingly) *The Favor of God*, was published by Regal Books and has been distributed worldwide. We even created a comprehensive, personal and small-group study curriculum for this book.

Finally, Jerry Savelle Ministries International had a complete and easy-to-understand resource that contained all the material we had on the biblical topic of God's favor.

Or so I thought.

Over the following months, as I continued to teach the Body of Christ about the favor of God, my study of His Word revealed new insights. The one that was most significant to me was revealed as I read this passage of scripture from the book of Zechariah: "And I will pour out on the house of David and on the inhabitants of Jerusalem the Spirit of grace and supplication" (Zechariah 12:10 AMP). I'd read this verse many times before, but this time the words "the Spirit of grace" caught my attention in a new way.

The words *grace* and *favor* are synonymous when they appear in the Bible. Any time we read the word grace in a passage of scripture, we can accurately replace it with *favor*. That's why the Amplified Bible translates Zechariah 12:10 like this: "And I will pour out upon the house of David and upon the inhabitants of Jerusalem the Spirit of grace or unmerited favor and supplication." In other words, God said a time was coming when He would pour out the Spirit of favor. But what exactly is the Spirit of favor?

In the Old Testament, the word *spirit* is derived from the original word *ruwach*. It means "wind, breath, or life." The first time this word appears in the Bible is in the book of Genesis:

> In the beginning God created the heavens and the earth. The earth was without form, and void; and darkness was on the face of the deep. And the Spirit of God was hovering over the face of the waters.
>
> Then God said, "Let there be light"; and there was light.
>
> (Genesis 1:1–3)

Notice that something happened when the Spirit of God came into contact with darkness. God declared the existence of light, and light came forth.

In addition to meaning "wind, breath, and life," the word ruwach also means "resemblance; a rational being including its expression and functions." In the beginning, the Spirit of God was the very resemblance of God Himself, expressed and functioning as the Creator. God said, "Let there be light," and there was light.

In the New Testament, the word *spirit* is derived from the Greek word *pneuma*, which means "wind; mental disposition."

Throughout the Bible, the word *spirit* is attached to numerous expressions, functions, and dispositions—both good and bad. The Bible talks about the spirit of life, the spirit of wisdom, the spirit of truth, as well as familiar spirits, a lying spirit, and a jealous spirit. In each instance, the spirit functions just as its name suggests. Likewise, the

Spirit of favor functions just as its name suggests.

In my book *The Favor of God*, we spent time examining the blessing of God conferred upon mankind in the beginning. The word *blessing* means "empowered to prosper." We learned that wherever the blessing of God is in operation, the favor of God is also present to bring about the opportunities to prosper.

Don't be concerned if you haven't yet read *The Favor of God*. Chapter 1 of this book, *The Spirit of Favor on Your House*, provides an overview of the key topics found in *The Favor of God*, including a study of our heritage of favor and the importance of declaring God's favor. You'll also enjoy learning about the ten specific benefits we can come to expect when we make walking in God's favor our lifestyle.

As we progress through *The Spirit of Favor* on Your House, you'll learn the difference between the *conferred* blessing of God and the *commanded* blessing of God that was promised to all who would obey Him. You'll see how the blessing and favor work hand in hand to prosper those who are willing to apply these biblical truths to their lives.

You will also come to understand how the Spirit of favor functions in the life of a believer, providing a wall of protection around his or her house—the entirety of that person's earthly existence and influence. And I'll present a biblical picture of the house upon which the Spirit of favor has been poured out.

Let me be clear: Just because the Spirit of favor has been poured out upon our house doesn't mean we will never face adversity. As long as we are alive and living on this earth, we will have adversity. But we do not have to be overcome by it.

Joseph was a man who knew the adversity of slavery and imprisonment, yet we will see in the final chapter of this book how the favor of God that was upon Joseph enabled him to flourish throughout every phase of his life. And in the end, the favor of God even restored Joseph to his loving father, Jacob, who had long thought him dead.

I can only imagine the joy and wonder Jacob must have felt when he saw his son, now an adult and the governor of Egypt. I also am a father of two adult children. My daughters are both grown and married, and have blessed me with seven grandchildren—but they are still my little girls as far as I'm concerned.

I started this ministry when my daughters were young; they grew up with a daddy who preached and traveled all over the world. In those early days, before I would leave to preach, I'd go into their room while they were still sleeping and place an envelope filled with change on the table between their beds. I'd write on the envelope, "Terri and Jerri—Daddy loves you. Here's some pocket change for you to spend while Daddy's gone." I loved pouring out my love and favor upon my girls.

Well, it's been more than forty years since I used to leave them envelopes filled with change, and I still enjoy giving them envelopes filled with pocket money. The only difference between then and now is that the amount of money has increased considerably. They say, "Daddy, you don't have to do this. We have jobs; we earn money."

I tell them, "I can't help it. Every time I think of you, I want to bless you."

My older daughter and her husband were in the process of buying a new home when they discovered they didn't have quite enough money to make it happen. I said, "I can help; I can make it happen."

"No, Daddy," she said. "We're not going to let you do it."

"Why not?" I asked. "I can help you, so let me do it."

"No, Daddy," she insisted, "you don't need to do this."

So I said, "Okay then, if you don't want the money, I'll just give it to your sister."

That's when she said, "Well, wait a minute. Let's pray about it."

I can't help wanting to be a blessing to my daughters. That's just the way good daddies are. We have a heavenly Father who wants to do the same for us. He wants to bless us. He wants us to flourish in the life He's given us. That's why He's already poured out His Spirit of favor upon us.

Because of the redemptive work Jesus Christ did at Calvary, offering His holy blood as atonement for our sins, the Bible says that we can now "fearlessly and confidently and boldly draw near to the throne of grace (the throne of God's unmerited favor to us sinners)" (Hebrews 4:16 AMP). Sadly, not everyone will accept God's gift of redemption. The Bible says, "Anyone who has rejected Moses' law dies without mercy on the testimony of two or three witnesses. Of how much worse punishment, do you suppose, will he be thought worthy who has trampled the Son of God underfoot, counted the blood of the covenant by which he was sanctified a common thing, and insulted the Spirit of grace [favor]?" (Hebrews 10:28–29).

I have no intention of rejecting any gift from God that was paid for by the precious blood of Jesus. Instead, like Paul, I intend to lay hold of that for which Christ Jesus has also laid hold of me, pressing toward the prize of the upward call of God in Christ Jesus (see Philippians 3:12–14).

I invite you to join me now to explore a biblical perspective of what to expect when the Spirit of favor is on your house.

CHAPTER 1

UNDERSTANDING THE FAVOR OF GOD

Oftentimes, people tend to blame God when they do not see their prayers being answered *when* they want them answered and in the way they expect them to be answered. I've been asked, "Brother Jerry, why isn't God listening to me? Why isn't He doing something? What's the problem?"

My answer is always, "God is not the problem. The problem is a lack of understanding."

Most of the time, the reason we experience delays in our prayers being answered is that we do not have an understanding of the power of the favor of God. And without an understanding of the favor of God, we will not appropriate it and confess it on a consistent basis. In order to understand the favor of God, we first need to understand the meaning of the word *favor,* of which there are four definitions.

The first definition of *favor* is "something granted out of goodwill." In other words, the favor of God is granted out of His goodwill toward us. It's not something that can be bought, and it's not something that can be earned. God's favor belongs to us because of the price Jesus

17

paid on the cross, and we are therefore entitled to walk in it.

The second definition of *favor* is "a gift bestowed as a token of regard, love, or friendliness." Have you ever asked someone, "Would you do me a favor?" What you're actually asking is, "Would you bestow on me a gift or a token of our friendship?" That's what *favor* is, a token of friendship.

The third definition of *favor* is simply "preferential treatment." We already know we have the *favor* of God, but according to His Word, we also have favor with man: "But let your heart keep my commands; for length of days and long life and peace they will add to you. Let not mercy and truth forsake you; bind them round your neck, write them on the tablet of your heart, and so find favor and high esteem in the sight of God and man" (Proverbs 3:1–3).

The fourth definition of *favor* is "advantage." To have an advantage means we have something working for us that others may not have working for them. For believers, we know it is the favor of God.

Getting a revelation of the favor of God can change every negative circumstance and situation a person may be facing; yet the very revelation of God's favor comes first through a revelation of Jesus Christ.

The Word of God says, "Therefore gird up the loins of your mind, be sober, and rest your hope fully upon the grace that is to be brought to you at the revelation of Jesus Christ" (1 Peter 1:13). The Amplified Bible text of this verse says, "Set your hope wholly . . . on the grace (divine favor) that is coming to you."

Notice that the New King James text uses the word *grace*, which the Amplified Bible translates as "divine favor." The Hebrew word for grace is *chen*, which is defined as "favor, kindness, and graciousness."

So as you read and study God's Word, anytime you see the word grace, stop and translate it as "divine favor," and then meditate on that verse. When we stop and translate it as such, Scripture takes on a whole new meaning.

> GETTING A REVELATION OF THE **FAVOR OF GOD** CAN CHANGE **EVERY** NEGATIVE CIRCUMSTANCE AND SITUATION

DECLARING GOD'S FAVOR

It's not enough just to have a revelation of the importance of God's favor—that is, just to think the favor of God is important. We also need a revelation of the importance of *declaring* that favor. There's a divine connection between our declaring the favor of God and the subsequent manifestation of it. Not a day goes by in which I'm not declaring the favor of God over my life, whether I'm believing God for an airplane or looking for a parking space.

Most of us face challenges (both large and small) on a regular basis, oftentimes referring to the larger challenges as *mountains*. Take debt, for instance. When we're facing a mountain of debt, that mountain will talk to us. It will keep us up all night, trying to convince us it's too big to deal with and that it's been with us too long for us ever to get rid of it. Truth be told, in the natural we don't have the ability to change the situation. But Jesus said we have to talk to our mountains: "For assuredly, I say to you, whoever says to this mountain, 'Be removed and cast into the sea,' and does not doubt in his heart, but believes those things he says will be done, he will have whatever he says" (Mark 11:23).

You may be wondering what God's favor has to do with mountains. We're all familiar with the verse in Zechariah that says, "'Not by might nor by power, but by My Spirit,' says the LORD of hosts" (Zechariah 4:6). Most of us stop reading at this point, but let's see what verse 7 says: "Who are you, O great mountain? Before Zerubbabel you shall become a plain! And he shall bring forth the capstone with shouts of 'Grace, grace to it!'"

According to the Word of God, we are to shout *grace*, or *God's favor*, to our mountain. When we declare and shout divine favor to our mountain, what we are doing is speaking words of faith, just as Jesus said we should do. We're expressing our faith in the favor of God to move that mountain.

The apostle Paul's revelation of favor became a revelation of the power of *declaring* that favor over the lives of those he ministered to. He wrote thirteen of the twenty-seven epistles, or letters, contained in the New Testament. In each one he began with a greeting of grace, or divine favor, and usually concluded with a reminder to his readers that the grace of the Lord Jesus Christ would be with them all.

In his letter to the Romans, Paul wrote, "Grace [divine favor] to you and peace from God our Father and the Lord Jesus Christ" (Romans 1:7). To the church at Corinth he also said, "Grace [divine favor] to you and peace from God our Father and the Lord Jesus Christ" (1 Corinthians 1:3; 2 Corinthians 1:2). Concluding his letter to the Galatians, Paul wrote, "The grace [divine favor] of our Lord Jesus Christ be with your spirit. Amen" (Galatians 6:18).

Time and time again, we see Paul declaring God's favor over the Church, the Body of Christ. He was endeavoring to cause them to get a revelation of God's favor. He wanted them to understand that the favor of God brings with it blessing, prosperity, and victory over every adversity. He wanted them to understand they didn't have to be poor anymore, they didn't have to be sick anymore, and they didn't have to live "under the circumstances."

Neither do we.

A HERITAGE OF FAVOR

Before God ever spoke forth the words "let there be light," setting in motion the creation of all things that exist, He had a marvelous plan for mankind. The Bible tells us God's plan was that all people would be redeemed by faith, as Paul explained in his letter to the Galatians.

And the Scripture, foreseeing that God would justify the Gentiles by faith, preached the gospel to Abraham beforehand, saying, "In you all the nations shall be blessed." So then those who are of faith are blessed with believing Abraham.

For as many as are of the works of the law are under the curse; for it is written, "Cursed is everyone who does not continue in all things which are written in the book of the law, to do them." But that no one is justified by the law in the sight of God is evident, for "the just shall live by faith." Yet the law is not of faith, but "the man who does them shall live by them."

(Galatians 3:8–12)

The covenant God made with Abraham extended to both his natural and his spiritual posterity. Abraham's natural lineage included his son Isaac and his grandson Jacob, who later became Israel, for whom the whole Hebrew nation is named. The term *Gentile* applies to all non-Jewish people, tribes, and nations. And it is by faith in Jesus Christ that Gentiles become the spiritual seed of Abraham, as Paul goes on to explain.

Christ has redeemed us from the curse of the law, having become a curse for us (for it is written, "Cursed is everyone who hangs on a tree"), that the blessing of Abraham might come upon the Gentiles in Christ Jesus, that we might receive the promise of the Spirit through faith.

Now to Abraham and his Seed were the promises made. He does not say, "And to seeds," as of many, but as of one, "And to your Seed," who is Christ.

And if you are Christ's, then you are Abraham's seed, and heirs according to the promise.

(Galatians 3:13–14, 16, 29)

If you and I belong to Christ, if we've made Jesus the Lord of our lives, the Bible says we are Abraham's seed and heirs according to the promise. In other words, whatever God promised to Abraham, He has also promised to us, as we see in Romans 4:16: "Therefore it is of faith that it might be according to grace [divine favor], so that the promise might be sure to all the seed." The apostle Paul is telling us these promises are "sure" to the seed. The word sure means "certain, unfailing, or infallible." We could say that God's promises are a sure thing.

Genesis 12 contains a particular promise God made to Abraham that applies to us as heirs of the promise. God said, "I will make you a great nation; I will bless you and make your name great; and you shall be a blessing" (Genesis 12:2). The Amplified version of this scripture says, "I will bless you [with abundant increase of favors]." In other words, God is promising to increase His favor in Abraham's life. And as we follow Abraham's story, we see that God's favor indeed caused him to become a very prosperous man.

An abundant increase in favor brought good things into Abraham's

> WHATEVER GOD PROMISED TO **ABRAHAM**, HE HAS ALSO PROMISED TO **US**

life, and it will bring good things to us, as well. This kind of abundant favor is our heritage; it is available for us because we are the seed of Abraham. And we have an even more sure promise of favor because the Word tells us that God "is able to do exceedingly abundantly above all that we ask or think" (Ephesians 3:20).

In other words, there are benefits that come when we are walking in the favor of God.

TEN BENEFITS OF WALKING IN GOD'S FAVOR

In the more than forty years that I've been studying and walking in the favor of God, I've come to identify ten specific benefits I've experienced repeatedly in my personal life. I'm not just putting forth anecdotal information here; each one of these benefits is biblically based.

1. We will experience supernatural increase and promotion.

The life of Joseph, which we will examine in the final chapter of this book, gives us a clear picture of this aspect of God's favor. Because God's favor was upon him, after being sold into slavery by his brothers, he was placed in charge of everything his master possessed. The Bible says that the Lord blessed the house of the Egyptian for Joseph's sake.

Later, when Joseph was imprisoned after being falsely accused, he found favor with the keeper of the prison and was put in charge of the prisoners. But Joseph's story doesn't end there. He went on to become governor of Egypt, overseeing all the wealth and commerce in the land.

2. *We will experience the restoration of everything the enemy has stolen from us.*

God's people had been captives in Egypt for 430 years when He spoke these words to Moses: "And I will give this people favor in the sight of the Egyptians; and it shall be, when you go, that you shall not go empty-handed. But every woman shall ask of her neighbor, namely, of her who dwells near her house, articles of silver, articles of gold, and clothing; and you shall put them on your sons and on your daughters. So you shall plunder the Egyptians" (Exodus 3:21–22).

God didn't intend for His people to walk out of captivity empty-handed. That's why He said they would *plunder* the Egyptians, which means "to spoil, to recover, to rescue, and to snatch away." But notice that the people had a part to play in this restoration; they had to put a demand on God's favor by *asking* for those things God had promised them.

We, too, can put a demand on favor by making this declaration: "The favor of God will restore to me everything the enemy has stolen!"

3. *We will receive honor—even in the midst of our adversaries.*

As a result of the ninth plague released against Egypt, the land had just experienced three days of what the Bible describes as a thick darkness that could be felt. Yet Moses and the children of Israel had light in their dwellings throughout those three days. The Bible says, "And the LORD gave the people favor in the sight of the Egyptians. Moreover the man Moses was very great in the land of Egypt, in the sight of Pharaoh's servants and in the sight of the people" (Exodus 11:3).

Perhaps the most widely recognized of the psalms is the Twenty-third Psalm. We have all read these words penned by David: "You prepare a table before me in the presence of my enemies" (Psalm 23:5). David was not the first person to experience honor in the presence of his enemies. He may have been inspired by the story of what God did for Moses and the Israelites.

God has said, "I am the LORD, I do not change" (Malachi 3:6); therefore, we know that what He has done for Moses and for David, He will most certainly do for us as His favor brings us honor in the midst of our adversaries.

4. We will increase in assets, especially in the area of land and real estate.

Following the death of Moses, God told Joshua to arise and take the people across the Jordan into the land He was giving them. He said, "Every place that the sole of your foot will tread upon I have given you, as I said to Moses" (Joshua 1:3). Just as God had promised, He delivered the land into their hands—and they didn't have to fight for it. God said, "I delivered them into your hand. I sent the hornet before you which drove them out before you" (Joshua 24:11–12).

When we declare that God's favor will manifest as an increase in land and real estate, it happens. And guess what? We don't have to pay the world's price for it, either.

5. We will experience great victories in the midst of great odds.
One of the thing's I've come to understand about walking in the favor of God is that the more impossible the battle looks, the easier the victory will come. That's what happens when God's favor is upon us. When speaking of the armies gathered against Israel, the Bible says, "And the LORD delivered them into the hand of Israel, who smote them and chased them. For it was of the LORD to harden their hearts, that they should come against Israel in battle, that he might destroy them utterly, and that they might have no favour" (Joshua 11:8, 20 KJV).

Although the enemy armies surrounding the Israelites were a multitude that possessed countless horses, chariots, and presumably vast weapons of war, there was one thing they did not possess: *favor.* When the favor of God is upon us, we can expect to experience great victories in the midst of the greatest of odds.

6. We will receive recognition even when we may be the least likely to be selected.
As a boy, David was the youngest and the smallest of the sons of Jesse, from whom the prophet Samuel was to anoint a new king. When Jesse presented his sons to the old prophet, at first he didn't even include David. But when the young boy arrived, the Lord said to Samuel,

"Arise, anoint him; for this is the one!" (1 Samuel 16:12).

After being anointed, David went back to tending his father's sheep, but it wasn't long before Saul, the reigning king, sought him out. "So David came to Saul and stood before him. And he loved him greatly, and he became his armorbearer. Then Saul sent to Jesse, saying, 'Please let David stand before me, for he has found favor in my sight'" (1 Samuel 16:21–22).

When the favor of God is upon us, we will be recognized. All we have to do is confess that favor to ourselves and praise God for it. When we do, it won't be long before we receive recognition—even if we're the least likely to be selected.

7. We will experience preferential treatment.

I've learned that if we will come before God with a humble spirit, He will lift us up and give us preferential treatment.

The Bible says, "Humble yourselves under the mighty hand of God, that He may exalt you in due time" (1 Peter 5:6). That is just what had happened centuries earlier to a young woman named Esther who was taken before the king. "And Esther obtained favor in the sight of all who saw her. The king loved Esther more than all the other women, and she obtained grace and favor in his sight more than all the virgins; so he set the royal crown upon her head and made her queen" (Esther 2:15, 17).

Esther obtained favor and, as a result, was beloved by the king, who made her his queen. When the favor of God is on our lives, prominence and preferential treatment come right along with it.

8. Our petitions will be granted—even by ungodly civil authorities.

After learning of Haman's evil plot to kill all of the Jews in the kingdom, Esther formulated her own plan to petition the king for the lives of her people.

The Bible says, "At the banquet of wine the king said to Esther, 'What is your petition? It shall be granted you. What is your request, up to half the kingdom? It shall be done!' Then Esther answered and said, 'My petition and request is this: If I have found favor in the sight of the king, and if it pleases the king to grant my petition and fulfill my request, then let the king and Haman come to the banquet which I will prepare for them, and tomorrow I will do as the king has said'" (Esther 5:6–7).

Although the king did not worship the God of the Jews—the God of Abraham, Isaac, and Jacob—he was willing to grant Esther's petition because the favor of God rested upon her.

9. Policies, rules, and laws will be changed or reversed to our advantage.

The decree calling for the death of all Jews had already gone forth, and the date had been set. Yet because of the favor of God that rested upon Esther, a new decree went forth. "Then King Ahasuerus said to Queen Esther and Mordecai the Jew, 'Indeed, I have given Esther the house of Haman, and they have hanged him on the gallows because he tried to lay his hand on the Jews. You yourselves write a decree concerning the Jews, as you please, in the king's name, and seal it with the king's signet ring; for whatever is written in the king's name and sealed with the king's signet ring no one can revoke'"(Esther 8:4–8).

Notice that not only did the king agree to set forth a new decree, but also he allowed Esther and her cousin Mordecai to write the decree as they pleased, and then they sealed it with the king's own signet ring. The Bible goes on to say, "In every province and city, wherever the king's command and decree came, the Jews had joy and gladness, a feast and a holiday" (Esther 8:17).

10. We won't have to fight some battles, because God will fight them for us.
Most of us are familiar with the words young David spoke to the Philistine giant before killing him with a stone: "You come to me with a sword, with a spear, and with a javelin. But I come to you in the name of the LORD of hosts, the God of the armies of Israel. Then all this assembly shall know that the LORD does not save with sword and spear; for the battle is the LORD's" (1 Samuel 17:45, 47).

When we put our faith in God and His great favor, He will fight our battles for us. That's not to say we will never have to take a stand and exercise our faith, but we will certainly never have to fight our battles in our own strength. The psalmist wrote, "For they did not gain possession of the land by their own sword. Nor did their own arm save them; but it was Your right hand, Your arm, and the light of Your countenance, because You favored them" (Psalm 44:1–3).

∎∎∎

Coming to the place where we have knowledge and understanding of God's favor and what it takes to tap into that favor in a way that will produce benefits in our life is just the beginning. Simon Peter penned these words to believers:

> Grace [divine favor] and peace be multiplied to you in the knowledge of God and of Jesus our Lord.
>
> For if these things are yours and abound, you will be neither barren nor unfruitful in the knowledge of our Lord Jesus Christ.
>
> Therefore, brethren, be even more diligent to make you call and election sure, for if you do these things you will never stumble.
>
> (2 Peter 1:2, 8, 10)

When God called Abraham to leave his country, his family, and his father's house, He made this declaration: "I will bless you and make your name great; and you shall be a blessing" (Genesis 12:2). The Amplified Bible says, "I will bless you [with abundant increase of favors] and make your name famous and distinguished."

It is vital to understand that blessing and favor are inseparable.

CHAPTER 2

EMPOWERED TO PROSPER, FAVORED WITH OPPORTUNITY

Where we find the blessing, we always find favor. They are knit intricately together; we can't have the blessing of God without also having the favor of God.

To be blessed is to have the power to prosper and succeed. That's what blessed means: empowered to prosper. The blessing is an empowerment from God, who, in essence, said to Abraham, "I will empower you to prosper, to succeed. Not only that, but I'm going to give you an abundant increase of favors." The major characteristic of the covenant is the blessing, and the major characteristic of the blessing is favor.

When we study the Old Testament closely, we discover that people truly understood the power of the blessing; it was something they desired deeply and wanted on their lives. Those like Esau, who did not place a value on it, forfeited it. Those who understood it sought it. David petitioned the Lord, saying, "For You, O my God, have revealed to Your servant that You will build him a house. Therefore Your servant has found it in his heart to pray before You. And now, LORD, You are God, and have promised this goodness to Your servant. Now You have been pleased to bless the house of Your servant" (1 Chronicles 17:25–27).

David clearly understood the power of the blessing; it was something he desired. He knew that the blessing on a person's life, on a person's house, literally guaranteed prosperity, success, and total victory—no matter what was happening around them.

During a time of prayer, the Lord asked me this question: "Son, if the blessing is the empowerment to prosper and succeed, then what is My favor for?" Before I could respond, He gave me the answer: "Favor produces the opportunities to make the blessing happen."

It's one thing to be blessed with certain abilities, giftings, talents, and empowerments, but if an individual never gets the opportunity to tap into them and use them, what good are they? Perhaps a young athlete has been blessed with the ability to achieve a batting record equal to or better than that of Babe Ruth or Hank Arron. But if an opportunity never arises for him or her to play—or worse yet, an opportunity arises, but they don't seize it—then they've missed out on the very blessing God had prepared especially for them.

That's how it is for many Christians. They go through life with this tremendous ability and empowerment that came from heaven itself: the ability to prosper, to succeed, to increase, to multiply, to excel, to rise above. Even though they are blessed, they never tap into the blessing. They live way beneath their privileges as children of God, never experiencing all that God has laid in store for them. I believe when these Christians get to heaven, they are going to see everything they could have had here on earth—if only they had seized the opportunities God placed before them.

Years ago, my son-in-law Rodney saw an ad in the paper for an old video game that was broken. He bought it, repaired it, and sold it for more money

> "FAVOR PRODUCES THE **OPPORTUNITIES** TO MAKE THE **BLESSING** HAPPEN."

that he had bought it for. He realized there was a demand for these old video games, so he began a business of buying and selling them. Rodney eventually became the number one arcade game distributor in Texas, and it all started with an opportunity. What if he had said, "I don't want to have to work on the game to fix it, God—just give me one that works"? He would have missed the opportunity God's favor had sent his way. I'm convinced the reason many believers don't prosper is this: when an opportunity comes their way, it doesn't come in the form they expect.

It's like the man whose home is in the path of a hurricane. He's been told to evacuate, but he won't do it. The water is rising, and he's moved to the roof of his house where he's determined to trust God to rescue him. People are passing by in boats, trying to persuade him to get in, but he says, "No, I'm just trusting in God." In a little while, a helicopter flies over and drops a basket down to him. He says he won't get in because he's trusting God. Well, he drowns and goes to heaven. When he sees God he says, "God, I'm disappointed in You. I was trusting You to rescue me, and You didn't do it." God replied, "I sent a boat and a helicopter. What else did you want?"

Thomas Edison once said, "The reason so many people miss opportunities is that they often come dressed in work clothes." I've found this to be true in my own life with the homes Carolyn and I have purchased. When we bought our first small home, it was what you'd call a fixer-upper. We worked to improve it, and as a result, we doubled our money when we sold it. We followed this pattern on subsequent homes we owned until the time came when we built our dream home, which today is completely paid for. The ability to prosper has been with us all along. What we needed was opportunity, and that's just what the favor of God provided.

> THE REASON MANY BELIEVERS **DON'T PROSPER** IS THIS: WHEN AN OPPORTUNITY COMES THEIR WAY, IT DOESN'T COME IN THE **FORM THEY EXPECT**.

So many Christians are satisfied with survival mode. "We have enough to pay our bills, with just a little left over," they say. Getting by with a little left over is okay, but tapping into the prosperity that the blessing produces is better.

In Genesis 12:2, God said to Abraham, "I will bless you." And in

Genesis 13:2, we see that Abraham "was very rich in livestock, in silver, and in gold." It only took one chapter for the blessing to make him a rich man. I like what the book of Proverbs says: "The blessing of the LORD makes one rich" (Proverbs 10:22).

The blessing of God will bring prosperity into a believer's life for a reason; it's not just so that we can live well. God doesn't mind our living well, but prosperity has a greater purpose. When God told Abraham that He would bless him, He also declared in the same sentence that he would be a blessing: "I will bless you and make your name great; and you shall be a blessing" (Genesis 12:2).

The primary reason for our being blessed and empowered to prosper is so that we can be a blessing to others. We are blessed to further the kingdom of God, to help people in need, and to help send missionaries around the world. The blessing is what enables us to help the widow, the orphan, the poor, the destitute, and the people who don't know these things. This is what the blessing is all about. The more we tap into the blessing of God, the more prosperity we will experience, which enables us to do more for other people and the kingdom of God.

I couldn't do everything I do around the world if I didn't believe in the power of blessing of God. Jerry Savelle Ministries International is on television in two hundred nations; we plant churches and Bible schools, and we sow into other people and ministries who are also advancing the kingdom of God.

There is nothing more fun than being a blessing, nothing more exciting than being a giver. I say this to the glory of God: Carolyn and I do not have any debt except our monthly utilities; our greatest household expense is our giving. There was a time when we were in need for somebody to bless us. When we first got into the Word of God, there were times when we didn't know where our next meal was coming from. We didn't know where we'd get money to put gas in the car. But those days are long gone.

> THE **PRIMARY REASON** FOR OUR BEING BLESSED AND EMPOWERED TO PROSPER IS SO THAT WE CAN **BE A BLESSING TO OTHERS**.

I have been rich, and I have been poor. Rich is better.

BLESSING AND FAVOR WORK HAND IN HAND

In the book of Psalms we find these words penned by David: "For You, O LORD, will bless the righteous; with favor You will surround him as with a shield" (Psalm 5:12). Notice how these two powerful forces of blessing and favor are directly linked together in this psalm. According to Psalm 3:8, we already have the blessing upon us: "Your blessing is upon Your people."

Remember, God's blessing is the empowerment to prosper, and favor produces opportunities for prosperity to happen. If I'm surrounded by favor, then I'm surrounded with opportunities to prosper. Once we understand that blessing and favor work hand in hand and that the blessing is already upon us, we can focus on seizing the opportunities God is sending our way.

I've actually had people say to me, "But you don't understand, Brother Jerry, I don't have a formal education in my field."

"It's not your education in your field that empowers you to prosper," I tell them. "It's the blessing of God!"

If you have made Jesus the Lord of your life, then you are capable of prospering. It doesn't matter what your background is, what your race or gender is, what part of town you grew up in, or the fact that nobody in your family has ever been prosperous. You already have the potential to prosper beyond what you've imagined.

ACTIVATING THE FAVOR OF GOD

Oral Roberts once said to me, "Miracles are coming your way every day; you either attract them, or they pass you by." Likewise, opportunities to prosper come our way every day, and we either attract them or let them pass us by. Some people call this principle the "law of attraction," which simply means we have the ability to attract certain things in our lives on the basis of our attitudes and the way we talk. This law is actually a biblical principle the world has taken hold of. They don't know it's a biblical principal; they just know it's working for them.

If the law of attraction will work for a non-believer, surely it will work for God's people.

Napoleon Hill didn't come up with the principle "think and grow rich." The Bible says, "For as [a man] thinks in his heart, so is he" (Proverbs 23:7). Hill's book may not have referred to this verse, but the principle is clearly from the Word of God. How we think about a situation has everything to do with the outcome; how we speak about a situation has everything to do with the outcome; and our attitude about a situation has everything to do with the outcome. That's why I continually declare, "I am surrounded with favor, and that favor produces opportunities for me to prosper!"

Speaking to a situation is a biblical principle. Jesus said, "For assuredly, I say to you, whoever says to this mountain, 'Be removed and be cast into the sea,' and does not doubt in his heart, but believes that those things he says will be done, he will have whatever he says" (Mark 11:23). When it comes to attracting opportunities to prosper, we have to be aggressive. The way we do this is by speaking it more and more frequently. The Bible says, "Faith comes by hearing, and hearing by the word of God" (Romans 10:17). So when you hear the Word of God coming out of your mouth all the time, your faith is going to grow, which will put you in a position to lay hold of the opportunities coming your way.

Let's look again at the Amplified Bible translation of Genesis 12:2: "And I will make of you a great nation, and I will bless you [with abundant increase of favors] and make your name famous and distinguished, and you will be a blessing [dispensing good to others]." Notice the words "abundant increase of favors." That's favors—plural. This wording assures us we won't just have one opportunity to prosper in our lifetime. No! If we blow it, we're not done; God will give us other opportunities. He is our loving and merciful heavenly Father who keeps opportunities coming our way. It is our responsibility to attract those opportunities by believing what God's Word says about favor and declaring it.

People tend to want to blame their failure on everybody else instead of taking responsibility for themselves. It's amazing how quick some are to take credit for their successes, but when it comes to their failures, it's easer to blame others: "It's my boss's fault," "My spouse is standing in my way," or "Well, I just don't get the breaks like everybody else does." Quit blaming everybody else and take responsibility for yourself. The quicker you do, the quicker you're going to move into God's best for your life.

> WHEN IT COMES TO **ATTRACTING** OPPORTUNITIES TO PROSPER, WE HAVE TO BE **AGGRESSIVE**.

The favor of God is continually producing opportunities; it's your responsibility to activate it.

WE CAN POSITION OURSELVES FOR OPPORTUNITY

We understand that God's blessing and His favor are divinely linked together. When the blessing comes on a person's life, so does the favor of God. We can actually position ourselves for opportunities to prosper, and one of the ways we do this is by tithing.

> "Bring all the tithes into the storehouse, that there may be food in My house, and try Me now in this," says the LORD of hosts, "if I will not open the windows of heaven and pour out for you such a blessing that there will not be room enough to receive it. And I will rebuke the devourer for your sakes."
>
> (Malachi 3:10–11)

If God is going to pour out blessing on those who tithe, then we know that right along with the blessing comes the favor of God. This means those who tithe faithfully are putting themselves in the position for more opportunities to prosper.

The only other time the phrase windows of heaven is used in the Bible is in reference to the days of Noah and the flood. The windows of heaven were opened and a deluge of water was poured out, covering the entire earth. There was an outpouring, an unstoppable downpour. Based on this example, it looks to me as if God is saying to the faithful tither, "I'm going to cause an outpouring of unstoppable opportunities to prosper."

In the above Malachi passage, God also said He would rebuke the devourer, Satan, so that he would not even be able to get involved in what a tither is doing.

The Malachi 3 promise of blessing and protection is what the faithful tither can expect. Notice I say the faithful tither. This is not a promise to the person who "tries" tithing and then quits. You may ask, "You mean I have to tithe?" You don't have to do anything that I say or the Bible says. If you are satisfied with where you are right now—perhaps in the same rut you've been in for years—then stop reading this book right now, and keep living that way if it makes you happy. Of course, that's not the way God wants you to live. He gave you a free will, and with it the opportunity to choose and make your own decisions. God won't make you do anything, but if you think you can ignore His Word and still experience His best, you're deceived.

I don't consider living by God's Word an obligation or a religious chore. I never approach the Word with the attitude that I have to do it. It is my privilege to order my life according to God's Word: I see what obedience will produce, and I want those kinds of results.

Early in our marriage Carolyn had given me a Bible to keep at my paint and body shop, but I never read it. I read Hot Rod Magazine and any material that would show me how to get maximum performance out of whatever automobile I owned at the time. I was always thinking, "What else can I do to this engine? What else can I do to the rear end? What else can I do so that the transmission will give me more horsepower?" I was interested in maximum performance, so that's the kind of stuff I read. I found that if I did what the experts said they did to get results, I could expect the same results, because they'd already proved it would work.

When I came to the Lord, I approached the Bible as if it was God's manual for high-performance living and maximum results. I started reading the Word with the same determination I'd read those hot rod magazines with. If the Bible said I was to watch the words that came out of my mouth, then I changed the way I talked. If it said I was to take authority over what I looked at and listened to because what I saw and heard would get into my heart, then I purposed to guard my heart.

> ## IT IS MY PRIVILEGE TO **ORDER MY LIFE** ACCORDING TO **GOD'S WORD**

When I came across the scripture in Malachi where God promises to pour out a blessing on those who tithe, I didn't say, "Oh, I don't want to do that." No! The way I saw it, the way to get maximum results from God's blessing was for me to tithe, so I became a tither. I've now been faithfully tithing for more than forty years, and I'm not even thinking about quitting. Tithing is like breathing for me: it's so engrained in me that I never even think about it. I just enjoy experiencing the results.

There are those who do not tithe because they see it as an Old Testament practice. Oral Roberts once said to me, "The difference be-

tween Old Testament tithing and New Testament tithing is this: my
tithe is no longer a debt I owe, but a seed I sow." I tithe, not because
it's a religious obligation; rather, my tithe is a seed I sow out of my re-
spect and love for God. If it weren't for God, I wouldn't have anything
to start with. I would be back where I was over forty years ago. Those
who tithe faithfully position themselves for opportunities to prosper.
I like the way the Amplified Bible says it:

> Let each one [give] as he has made up his own mind and pur-
> posed in his heart, not reluctantly or sorrowfully or under com-
> pulsion, for God loves (He takes pleasure in, prizes above other
> things, and is unwilling to abandon or to do without) a cheerful
> (joyous, "prompt to do it") giver [whose heart is in his giving].
>
> And God is able to make all grace (every favor and earthly
> blessing) come to you in abundance, so that you may always and
> under all circumstances and whatever the need be self-sufficient
> [possessing enough to require no aid or support and furnished
> in abundance for every good work and charitable donation].
>
> (2 Corinthians 9:7–8)

When God finds the person who is joyous about giving, a faithful
tither, He causes His grace and His favor to abound in that person's
life. If favor is abounding, then opportunities to prosper are also
abounding. This sounds like the outpouring God promised in Mala-

chi when He said He would open the windows of heaven.

The bottom line is this: God's got us covered; all that's required of us is to just do what He says to do. The blessing is already ours and favor is already ours. The two are divinely connected for the purpose of bringing us opportunities to prosper.

All we have to do is position ourselves to receive.

CHAPTER 3
THE COMMANDED BLESSING

I remember when I came across an interesting statement while reading Alexander MacLaren's *Expositions of the Holy Scripture*. A renowned preacher whose ministry spanned more than fifty years, McLaren said, "Happy and fortunate is the life that God's commanded blessing is upon." What caught my attention was the word commanded.

In my book *Every Day a Blessing Day*, we examined how God conferred the blessing upon Adam and Eve when He said, "Be fruitful and multiply; fill the earth and subdue it; have dominion over the fish of the sea, over the birds of the air, and over every living thing that moves on the earth" (Genesis 1:28). The word *confer* means "to bestow as a gift or favor; to honor." The word *command* has a very different meaning, as we see in this familiar passage of scripture:

"Now it shall come to pass, if you diligently obey the voice of the Lord your God, to observe carefully all His commandments which I command you today, that the Lord your God will set you high above all nations of the earth. And all these blessings shall come upon you and overtake you, because you obey the voice of the Lord your God:

"Blessed shall you be in the city, and blessed shall you be in the country.

"Blessed shall be the fruit of your body, the produce of your ground and the increase of your herds, the increase of your cattle and the offspring of your flocks.

"Blessed shall be your basket and your kneading bowl.

"Blessed shall you be when you come in, and blessed shall you be when you go out.

"The Lord will cause your enemies who rise against you to be defeated before your face; they shall come out against you one way and flee before you seven ways.

"The Lord will command the blessing on you in your storehouses and in all to which you set your hand, and He will bless you in the land which the Lord your God is giving you."

(Deuteronomy 28:1–8)

The Hebrew word translated as *command* in verse 8 literally means "to enjoin; to charge; to put in order." The blessing God conferred upon mankind in the garden was a gift of love. The *commanded* blessing is a decree, an authoritative order, that bears with it God's eternal purpose. Notice the Lord has commanded His blessing upon the obedient. If you are obedient, then this commanded blessing is for you. He will command His blessing on everything you set your hand to; He will command it on your storehouses; He will command it upon the land He has given you.

The New Living Translation says, "The LORD will guarantee a blessing on everything you do."

The Amplifed Bible says, "The Lord shall command the blessing upon you in your storehouse and in all that you undertake."

THE MESSAGE says, "God will order a blessing on your barns and workplaces." This means the blessing will be showing up on your job. As a result, you will qualify for things that other people don't have a clue about.

Let's look again at the word *command*, which we understand to be an authoritative directive or declaration. A command always comes from one who is superior, and God is obviously superior to us. He is the Creator; we are the creation. The Creator of the universe has commanded His blessing upon us. When God makes a command, then divine order is established. Divine order removes all doubt and confusion regarding a matter. Once God issues a command, the matter is settled; it's not up for vote or opinion.

If God commands His blessing, then no one can justifiably question it. The commanded blessing is a given, but it's our

> IF YOU ARE **OBEDIENT**, THEN THIS COMMANDED **BLESSING** IS FOR YOU.

responsibility to align ourselves with it, accept it as the will of God, and then never doubt it. We are supposed to be blessed; this is God's divine order for our lives.

When God commanded the light to shine out of darkness, saying, "Let there be light" (Genesis 1:3), darkness didn't stand up and say, "We don't want light." I like the literal Hebrew translation of Genesis 1:3, which says, "Light be, and light was." Darkness could not stop the light from shining. God has commanded His blessing upon you, and the curse has to give way.

Proverbs 26:2 says, "So a curse without cause shall not alight." The curse has no right to function in my life once the commanded blessing is on my life. If the curse shows up, it's because I opened the door somewhere. If I stay in obedience to God and don't open the door to the curse, I will live under the commanded blessing.

The Bible says, "By the word of the LORD the heavens were made" (Psalm 33:6). The New Living Translation says, "The LORD merely spoke, and the heavens were created," and THE MESSAGE says, "The skies were made by GOD'S command." Psalm 33 goes on to say in verse 9, "He spake, and it was done; he commanded, and it stood fast" (KJV), and in THE MESSAGE, "He spoke and there it was, in place the moment he said so."

Hebrews 11:3 tells us, "By faith we understand that the worlds were framed by the word of God." That's how powerful God's command is; He just says something, and it's so.

The psalmist declared this truth about God: "Your blessing is upon Your people" (Psalm 3:8). The blessing came upon me the day I bowed my knee and said, "Jesus is Lord." The blessing never comes off; I don't just hang it in the closet and try to make things happen myself.

There was a time in my life when I tried doing things myself

> WE ARE **SUPPOSED** TO BE BLESSED; THIS IS GOD'S **DIVINE ORDER** FOR OUR LIVES.

and I found out what it produced: very little. But after I got saved, I began confessing the blessing of Abraham was upon me. Even when it didn't look like the blessing was upon me, I confessed it day and night. I began to learn about the empowerment of the blessing, and as I studied God's Word and applied what I was learning to my life, Carolyn's and my lifestyle began to change.

The blessing is the empowerment for me to prosper succeed, and I'm going to wear it 24/7.

SETTING SIGHTS ON THE BLESSING

We just read Deuteronomy 28:8, in which the Lord says He will command the blessing on all we set our hand to. Verse 11 goes on to say, "And the LORD will grant you plenty of goods." THE MESSAGE says, "GOD will lavish you with good things."

Lavish means "to bestow in profusion." It also means "unsparing, over-generous, and characterized by extravagance." If this is how God wants to bless us, then the Body of Christ as a whole has been setting its sights too low. There is nothing wrong with extravagance. I'm not talking about being wasteful; there is a difference. God doesn't mind that we have the best. When we are walking in the blessing and favor of God, we can have the best and not have to pay the world's price for it.

I was looking at some suits in an upscale men's store one day when the owner recognized me from my television program. He said, "Brother Jerry, you put out some very good information. Tell you what I'll do: anything you want in my store, I'll give you 50 percent off." That's the blessing and favor of God working hand in hand.

Going back to Deuteronomy 28:11, we see that the New American Standard Bible says, "The LORD will make you abound in prosperity." This would imply having more than enough. What's the point in having more than enough? You can't use it all on yourself, which means you can help others with what you have. You get to be a blessing to other people. And being a blessing to others is the most fun you can ever have in your life.

The apostle Paul picks up on this in his letter to Timothy. Speaking of God, he says, "the living God, who gives us richly all things to enjoy" (1 Timothy 6:17). This tells me God is interested in meeting more than just my needs. The Bible says if I delight myself in the Lord, then He will even give me the desires of my heart (see Psalm 37:4). God has done things like this in my life, things that only He can do. He's the God who does exceedingly, abundantly above all we can ask or think. There are not many of my dreams or desires that God has not already fulfilled—always better than I dreamed it.

As a young boy I wanted to jump out of airplanes. When I went into the military in the 1960s, I was so small that I couldn't qualify to jump out of planes. After I went into the ministry, I didn't think about it anymore; it was just something I'd wanted to do as a kid. But when I turned fifty, I had the opportunity to go skydiving. It was a dream and a desire that had been birthed in me decades earlier, and God made it happen.

Another dream was to fly in a fighter jet, and my staff knew this. So once when I was in Australia, my staff arranged for me to fly in a fighter jet with the New Zealand Royal Air Force. What a thrill that was for me.

I had always wanted to go to the Indy 500, and God made that happen too. Everything I've ever dreamed of and wanted to do, God has made happen. He gives us richly all things to enjoy. THE MESSAGE says that

BEING A BLESSING TO OTHERS IS THE **MOST FUN** YOU CAN EVER HAVE IN YOUR LIFE.

God "piles on all the riches we could ever manage" (1 Timothy 6:17).

Psalm 45:2 says, "God has blessed you forever." No matter what is happening in the world around us, we can rise above it, because we have the blessing of God. Once God commands His blessing on you and your house, He intends for it to be there forever. But the sad part is, the blessing can be upon a house, and yet there are those who will never experience the benefits. We see this principal illustrated in the story of Jesus healing the paralyzed man.

> Now it happened on a certain day, as He was teaching, that there were Pharisees and teachers of the law sitting by, who had come out of every town of Galilee, Judea, and Jerusalem. And the power of the Lord was present to heal them.
>
> (Luke 5:17)

This verse tells us that healing and the anointing were in the house, yet we don't see one single person who was part of the religious group of Pharisees and teachers get healed. Not one. Although the power was there to heal them, those who were sitting right there hearing Jesus teach didn't tap into it. Consequently, none were healed. Someone did, however, get healed that day—but it wasn't one of them.

NO MATTER WHAT IS HAPPENING IN THE WORLD AROUND US, WE CAN RISE ABOVE IT, BECAUSE **WE HAVE THE BLESSING** OF GOD.

Then behold, men brought on a bed a man who was paralyzed, whom they sought to bring in and lay before Him. And when they could not find how they might bring him in, because of the crowd, they went up on the housetop and let him down with his bed through the tiling into the midst before Jesus.

(Luke 5:18–19)

When these men heard the power of God was in the house—that Jesus was in the house—they went and got their friend, put him on a stretcher, and took him to the Master. When they arrived, the house was so crowded, they couldn't get through the door or even through a window. But they didn't give up. They were so determined to tap into what was available for them that they carried their friend to the top of the house, tore a hole in the roof, and lowered him down to Jesus.

When He saw their faith He said to [the paralytic], "Man, your sins are forgiven you."
Immediately he rose up before them, took up what he had been lying on, and departed to his own house, glorifying God."

(Luke 5:20, 25)

Setting our sights on the commanded blessing requires that we have faith—the kind of faith we might call "roof-tearing-off faith." The moment those men lowered their friend to Jesus, we're told that He saw their faith. Faith moved Jesus then, and it still moves God today.

Once we've set our sights of faith on the commanded blessing, tapping into it requires that we put a demand on it.

PUT A DEMAND ON THE BLESSING

Putting a demand on the blessing requires us to deliberately exercise our faith to demand, or summon, it. The Bible tells us that God "calls things which do not exist as though they did" (Romans 4:17). The word *calls* also means "to summon."

When God created the heavens and the earth, at a time when darkness covered the face of the earth, He simply said, "Let there be light," and there was light. He summoned it. Since we are made in the image of God, it stands to reason that we too can operate just as He does. Jesus said, "For assuredly, I say to you, whoever says to this mountain, 'Be removed and be cast into the sea,' and does not doubt in his heart, but believes that those things he says will be done, he will have whatever he says" (Mark 11:23).

Having experienced living under the commanded blessing of God firsthand, I've identified six things we can do to put a demand on it.

First, we must be aware that the commanded blessing exists. That's why I began this chapter by sharing the difference between the blessing God originally conferred upon mankind, which most of us understand, and the commanded blessing, which requires obedience on our part to activate.

Second, we must believe the commanded blessing belongs to us—which we can do if we base our belief upon the Word of God. This chapter is filled with scriptures that support this truth.

Third, we must speak the blessing over our lives continually. The apostle Paul was quoting King David when he said, "According as it is written, I believed, and therefore have I spoken; we also believe, and therefore speak" (2 Corinthians 4:13 KJV). What both David and Paul are telling us is this: whatever we truly believe in our hearts is what we're going to speak. In other words, if we truly believe the commanded blessing of God is upon our life, we will speak it continually. Psalm 35:27 says, "Let them say continually, 'Let the Lord be magnified, who has pleasure in the prosperity of His servant.'"

Fourth, develop your faith in the blessing of God. You do this by reading scriptures or listening to teaching about the blessing, because the Bible tells us, "Faith comes by hearing, and hearing by the word of God" (Romans 10:17). If you do this consistently, next thing you know, you'll begin to expect the blessing to show up. Faith and expectancy go together. If you truly have faith, then you're going to expect results.

Fifth, expect the blessing of God to manifest in some way every day of your life. Jesus asked two blind men who had called out to Him, "Do you believe that I am able to do this?" (Matthew 9:28). When they answered yes, He touched their eyes and said, "According to your faith let it be to you" (Matthew 9:29), and they were instantly healed. The results they got were according to their expectancy; real Bible faith carries with it a positive expectancy.

Sixth, demonstrate an attitude of gratitude. We should show God we are grateful and appreciate the fact that He has commanded the blessing upon our life and house. Being grateful opens the door to unlimited potential. I know I never get tired of my daughters telling me how much they love and appreciate me. Likewise, there are times when I am overcome with gratitude and I just have to stop and thank my heavenly Father for the blessing He has commanded upon my life.

...

I like the statement Smith Wigglesworth made many years ago, that God could pass over a thousand men to find one with faith. Make up your mind you're going to be that one person. The Bible says, "The eyes of the LORD run to and fro throughout the whole earth, to shew himself strong in the behalf of them whose heart is perfect toward him" (2 Chronicles 16:9 KJV).

> FAITH AND EXPECTANCY **GO TOGETHER**. IF YOU TRULY HAVE FAITH, THEN YOU'RE GOING TO **EXPECT RESULTS**.

I discovered being *perfect* toward God doesn't mean never having made a mistake or having sinned. It means being "trustworthy, loyal, faithful, dependable, reliable, committed, and consecrated." When I learned this, I said, "I can be that! God, if you're looking for somebody who will be faithful and committed, search no more; I'm your man." You can be that person too. Just tell God, "Search no more— here I am!"

God does not take His commands lightly. Psalm 105:8 says, "He remembers His covenant forever, the word which He commanded, for a thousand generations." The New Living Translation says, "He always stands by his covenant—the commitment he made to a thousand generations." God remembers His covenant: "My covenant I will not break, nor alter the word that has gone out of My lips" (Psalm 89:34).

God has decreed His blessing upon us, and He's not going to change that decree. If He's not going to change it, then it's up to us to get in the flow by putting a demand on the blessing. God has commanded the blessing upon the lives of the obedient—and He never says something He doesn't commit Himself to.

CHAPTER 4

FAVOR ON OUR HOUSE

"You're the most selfish person I've ever met," was the last line of the note I found taped to the front door of my house at the lake, a place Carolyn and I had owned for nearly thirty years.

"You don't even know me," I thought. The man who wrote the note obviously couldn't know that I'd just written a check for $11,000 to someone who was about to lose his home. The note was full of profanity, and the angry writer had called me pretty much everything imaginable—all because I owned two houses. The bottom line is, he was mad because *the favor of God was on my house.*

Isn't it just like the devil to stir someone up like that? But I'm not going to stop living under God's blessing and favor just because there are those who don't understand it or like it. Jesus said in the tenth chapter of Mark that along with blessings come persecutions. As far as I'm concerned, I'm going to continue enjoying God's blessing and favor upon my house regardless of what the world thinks.

We know that along with the blessing, which empowers us to prosper, come favor and the opportunities it produces. If the commanded blessing is upon our house, then so is God's favor.

When we talk about the favor of God being upon our "house," we're not just talking about a physical dwelling. Our house also encompasses our land, our family, our job or business, and our entire sphere of influence.

The favor of God is not only on my house and everyone in it; it's even on my dog, who's the most blessed dog in Crowley, Texas. She was just a hungry stray who came up to our door, so we started feeding her. That's how she became part of our house. Our ministry headquarters is located next door, and our staff members bring her treats. She's so blessed that she can't even eat everything that's given to her. She brings the treats back home and buries them. That dog is extremely blessed and highly favored. I said to her, "Girl, when you picked our house, you picked the right place. The favor of the Lord is on our house."

> OUR HOUSE ALSO **ENCOMPASSES** OUR LAND, OUR FAMILY, OUR JOB OR BUSINESS, AND OUR **ENTIRE** SPHERE OF INFLUENCE.

God's favor follows us wherever we go. It's good to know, in times like these, God's got us covered.

He spoke through the prophet Isaiah and said, "Declaring the end from the beginning, and from ancient times things that are not yet done, saying, 'My counsel shall stand, and I will do all My pleasure'" (Isaiah 46:10). THE MESSAGE puts it this way: "From the very beginning telling you what the ending will be, all along letting you in on what is going to happen." This is how God operates. He tells us from the beginning what the end will be, giving us clues all along the way.

This is just what the Lord did when He declared, "And I will pour out upon the house of David and upon the inhabitants of Jerusalem the Spirit of grace or unmerited favor" (Zechariah 12:10). One of the major themes of the book of Zechariah is this: God never forgets His promises. The name Zechariah literally means "the Lord remembers."

The "house of David" encompassed every aspect of David's being, including his descendants. From a prophetic standpoint, this promise to pour out God's favor was fulfilled when Jesus went to Calvary. Because Jesus was from the lineage of David, He was part of the house of David. This is why He is referred to many times in the Bible as "the son of David." When we receive Jesus as our Savior and Lord, we become part of the house of David.

The Spirit of favor has been poured out on our house!

I want to demonstrate through the scriptures what we are entitled to when the favor of God is upon our house. Remember God's promise in Deuteronomy 28:8, that if His people would be obedient to Him and to His Word, then His blessing and favor would come upon them.

GOODLY HOUSES

When the favor of God is upon your house, it will enable you to build what Deuteronomy 8:12 refers to as "goodly houses." One translation calls them "nice houses," another "fine houses." *Fine* refers to something that is characterized by elegance.

God doesn't mind that we have an elegant house. In fact, when the favor of God is upon us, it will enable us to build a goodly, elegant, fine, nice house. A nice house is one that is built with skillfulness, which is the opposite of shoddy, cheap, and inferior.

The first house Carolyn and I lived in cost $4,800 in 1966, and we had to take out a loan to buy it. The place needed a lot of work. At the time, we didn't know anything about the favor of God being upon our house. We were living beneath our God-given privileges because we were ignorant of this truth. But the moment we found out about God's favor, we were like two bulls in a china shop; we were determined to lay hold of everything God had for us.

We saw in God's Word that when the favor of God is on our house, or life, we would build "goodly houses." This is what we were believing for: a house built with skillfulness and elegance. Now, it didn't happen overnight. It didn't happen in a matter of a few months or even a few years. But, praise God, today we live in an elegant house that is paid for—and we also have a home at the lake.

Carolyn and I are a long way from that little, shoddy place we first moved into. We don't live like we used to live. Not only are we blessed, we are also capable of being a blessing to others now. I attribute all this to God's faithfulness to His Word. He said He would command His blessing upon me, and He did. He said He would pour out His favor on my house, and He did.

My life is a whole different story now because of God's favor on my house, and it can be your story too.

FULL OF ALL GOOD THINGS

Not only will the favor of God enable us to have goodly houses, but, according to Deuteronomy 6:11, these houses will be "full of all good things." When the favor of God is on your house, then it will be filled with good things. THE MESSAGE says that we will live in "well-furnished houses," and the New Living Translation uses the term "richly stocked."

Back in the early days, Carolyn and I were learning to believe God to furnish our house, room by room and piece by piece. We knew the importance of sowing, so once a room was finished, we'd sow a piece of furniture to someone else, and believe God to furnish the next room. I remember coming home one evening to find all of our furniture gone in one of our rooms. When I asked Carolyn where it went, she said, "Well, I found somebody who was in worse shape than we are, so I gave it to them."

That act of sowing an entire room of furniture not only produced a harvest of new furniture for us, but it also set into motion a pattern of sowing and reaping that worked in concert with the favor of God that was on our house. And Carolyn certainly did her part. She read Proverbs 31 and saw how a godly woman builds her house. She started confessing Deuteronomy 6:11, declaring, "Our house is filled with good things!"

Today Carolyn and I live in a home where every wall is filled with good things; it is a home that is truly richly stocked and well furnished. As we've continued to sow, God has continued to fill our home with good things. This is the kind of home we should expect when the favor of God is on our house.

I've also learned that having a goodly house filled with good things will bring persecution. Jesus said when we receive houses and land in this lifetime, we also receive persecutions (see Mark 10:29–30). Nobody ever had anything ugly to say about me when I lived in the shoddy house; the persecution didn't begin until God's favor started working.

I've already told you about the note that was left at my lake house, but at another time there was this guy who would drive by my home on a regular basis. He apparently thought it was his call in life to stop in front of my house and accuse me of stealing the money it took to build it. "Hey, preacher," he'd say, "did you steal the money for the house? Did you steal the money for that car?"

T. L. Osborn once gave me a great piece of advice. "There are only two kinds of people in the world: those who cheer you and those who jeer you. You have to be careful of both," he said. "The ones who cheer you and worship the ground you walk on are dangerous too. If you listen to everything they say about you, it can create pride. As for those who jeer you, don't pay any attention to them. It's just their carnal way of saying, 'I wish I were you.'"

I was recently at a church, teaching about the favor of God, when a couple who had just sowed a financial seed approached me and asked me to pray with them about a new house they were believing God for. When I prayed for them, I said, "And, Lord, let it be a spacious house." I hadn't given any thought to praying that way; the words just came up out of my spirit.

Two months later I was at their church again, conducting a meeting. They said, "Brother Jerry, we could hardly wait for you to get here so that we could take you to see our new house. We want you to dedicate it." I, of course, agreed. When we got to the house, the first thing I noticed was that it was indeed a spacious house, a gorgeous place on a hill overlooking the city.

When I asked how God had brought it about, the husband said, "Let me tell you the story. After we sowed that seed, one day I was driving home from work and the Lord told me to look up and to the left. When I did, I saw a beautiful house on a hill. The Lord said, 'There's your spacious house.'"

My friend didn't know who lived in the house, but he drove up the hill, got out of his car, and knocked on the door. When a woman answered the door, he asked if the house might be for sale. She said, "No, it's not. This is our dream house, and we've only been in here a little over a year."

"Well, can I leave my name and number in case you decide to sell it?" he asked. She took his information out of courtesy. A few weeks later he was surprised when she called and asked him to come to the house. When he arrived, she and her husband explained they were Christians involved in helping missionaries in different parts of the world. She said, "We built this big house with the idea of providing missionaries with a nice place to stay while we take care of them. But I haven't been able to get my mind off the fact that you wanted to know if it was for sale."

"So, is it for sale?" he asked.

"No," she told him. "But we just wanted to tell you the story."

He left, but a few weeks later she called him again and told him how much the house was worth. That was all she said, no mention of wanting to sell. He said, "Thank you for calling."

The next time she called, she said, "We can't get you off our minds. I don't know why I'm doing this, but would you be interested in making an offer?" When he gave her a figure, she said, "I don't think we can do that, but I'll talk to my husband and get back to you."

When she called back, she said, "We think we built this house for you, and we accept your offer."

He told me, "Brother Jerry, to answer your question, the favor of God got us this house!"

Let me give you a hint to help you know when you are about to receive a manifestation of God's favor. Anytime someone says to you,

"I don't know why I'm doing this, but . . . ," start smiling—the favor of God is coming your way.

TREASURE IN THE HOUSE

In addition to having goodly houses filled with all good things, the home of the righteous will contain treasure. Proverbs 15:6 says, "In the house of the righteous there is much treasure, and Psalm 5:12 says, "For You, O LORD, will bless the righteous; with favor You will surround him as with a shield."

We see that the righteous ones who have the blessing and favor of God on their house will also have "much treasure." The Amplified Bible describes this abundance as "priceless treasure," which implies possessions that are highly prized and valuable. Carolyn has declared this scripture about "much treasure" for many years now, and I can tell you that our house is indeed filled with things that are highly prized and valuable to us. Carolyn particularly treasures her china and paintings; I treasure my classic cars.

But here's the beautiful thing: Carolyn and I made a solemn decision more than forty years ago when we first discovered the power of the blessing and the favor of God, and we didn't have anything. We

> THE RIGHTEOUS ONES WHO HAVE **THE BLESSING** AND FAVOR OF GOD ON THEIR HOUSE WILL ALSO HAVE "MUCH TREASURE"

said, "Lord, when your blessing and favor begin to fill our house with good things and treasure, we will purpose to become a clearinghouse, a distribution center. We will never allow any 'thing' to possess us; we will instead possess it, which means we will sow it whenever You ask us to."

I remember going to my garage one day and saying to the Lord, "Since I've been serving You, I've acquired the finest classic cars I've ever owned." The cars in my garage were better than the ones I had at the time when working on cars for a living was my "god." At the time, I thought I couldn't live without them and the pleasure they gave me.

I went on to say, "I gave all that up for You, for the gospel's sake, and in return You have blessed me with things that are much finer than I ever had. Lord, I want you to know that none of this means anything to me other than the fact that it all came from You. If You want me to sow these cars into somebody else's life, I'll do it before dark." Right then, the Lord told me who to give them to, and I immediately cleared out my garage. I gave away everything that was in it.

When I told Carolyn what I'd done, she said, "Jerry Savelle, God already knows that you don't let anything come between you and Him. Don't ever do that again! When you sow a whole garage full of cars, it will come back to you in a fleet." She was right; I had to build another garage. And today, I use them as a tool for evangelism through our Chariots of Light Christian Car Club.

A house that is filled with treasures implies wealth. The Bible says, "Great wealth is in the house of the righteous" (Proverbs 15:6 NASB), and of those who fear the Lord it says, "Wealth and riches will be in his house" (Psalm 112:3). THE MESSAGE says, "Their houses brim with wealth."

In spite of what God's Word teaches about wealth being in the house of the righteous, many Christians can't even say "wealth," much less live it. In the mind of those in some religious circles, being wealthy is a sign of sin or compromise.

Nevertheless, God has no problem with His people being wealthy as long as they always attribute their wealth, success, and prosperity to Him: "And you shall remember the LORD your God, for it is He who gives you power to get wealth" (Deuteronomy 8:18).

LIMITLESS FAVOR

God's favor is limitless. When the favor of God is on your house, prosperity will be ongoing—regardless of what's going on in the world. When everyone else is experiencing gloom, doom, despair, depression, sadness, fear, and hopelessness, the Amplified says, "He declares blessed (joyful and favored with blessings) the home of the just and consistently righteous" (Proverbs 3:33).

Even in times of famine, drought, lack, or a bad economy, listen to what Psalm 37:19 says of the upright, those who have the favor of God on their house: "They shall not be ashamed in the evil time, and in the days of famine they shall be satisfied." Being satisfied means to be "calm, at peace, or worry free." Other translations say that the righteous will have "more than enough"; they will have "abundance." THE MESSAGE says, "In hard times, they'll hold their heads high; when the shelves are bare, they'll be full." This is what happens when the limitless favor of God is on your house.

Because the favor of God is limitless, it is also progressive. Psalm 115:14 declares, "May the LORD give you increase more and more, you and your children." The phrase "more and more" implies being taken continually to a higher level. When others seem to be going under due to the many negative situations happening in the world around them, God declares that "the wicked are overthrown and are no more, but the house of the righteous will stand" (Proverbs 12:7).

Not only will the house of the righteous stand, it will also flourish. Proverbs 14:11 says, "The house of the wicked will be overthrown, but the tent of the upright will flourish." To flourish means to "make steady progress, increase, or thrive." Even in adversity, the favor of God on our house will cause us to flourish. We will be like the three Hebrew children when they came out of the fiery furnace: there was no evidence they'd even been near a fire. When the favor of God is on your house, even if you go through a period of adversity, you'll come out on the other side with no evidence of what you've experienced.

The favor of God upon our house provides a shield of protection. Psalm 91:10 says, "No evil shall befall you, nor shall any plague come near your dwelling." Through the prophet Isaiah, God said, "My people will dwell in a peaceful habitation, in secure dwellings, and in quiet resting places" (Isaiah 32:18).

When the favor of God is upon our house, we can experience a peaceful and undisturbed place. You might be asking, "How can I get that?"

EVEN IN **ADVERSITY**, THE FAVOR OF GOD ON OUR HOUSE WILL CAUSE US TO **FLOURISH**.

You already have it; it's already there. Stop trying to get something that already belongs to you. Settle this truth in your heart, and declare with me, "The favor of God is on my house!"

CHAPTER 5

A HEDGE OF FAVOR

In the twenty-fourth chapter of Matthew, Jesus answered His disciples' question about the end of the world by describing a time filled with trouble and chaos, a time when there would be wars and rumors of wars, a time marked by lawlessness, famines, and earthquakes in various places. All we have to do is turn on the evening news to see that we are living in that time.

Interestingly, in the midst of Jesus' description of a world run amok, He made this amazing statement: "See that you are not troubled, for all these things must come to pass" (Matthew 24:6). Jesus was saying that it is possible to live in a world filled with trouble and chaos, and yet not be troubled by it. But how can this be? We find the answer in the prayer Jesus prayed in the company of His disciples preceding His crucifixion:

> "But now I come to You, and these things I speak in the world, that they may have My joy fulfilled in themselves. I have given them Your word; and the world has hated them because they are

not of the world, just as I am not of the world. I do not pray that You should take them out of the world, but that You should keep them from the evil one."

(John 17:13–15)

This is a prayer from Jesus to the Father. Jesus doesn't have much time left on earth. He is preparing to become the sacrificial Lamb to redeem mankind, yet He prays that His followers will have His joy.

A lot of times when we hear people, especially the religious-minded, talk about Jesus, they don't say much about His joy. Instead, they focus on His being a man of sorrow. We know He did experience sorrow, because the Bible tells us He wept over the condition of Israel. They were scattered; they had allowed religious tradition to make the Word of God of no effect in their lives; they had constantly missed the visitation of the Lord. Even so, Jesus didn't go around crying all the time. He wasn't the lowly, weak, sad man that religious tradition portrays. He was a man of joy. The Bible says, "The joy of the LORD is your strength" (Nehemiah 8:10). Clearly, Jesus was a man of joy.

I especially like the way the Amplified Bible translates John 17:13: "And now I am coming to You; I say these things while I am still in the world, so that My joy may be made full and complete and perfect in them [that they may experience My delight fulfilled in them, that My enjoyment may be perfected in their own souls, that they may have My gladness within them, filling their hearts]."

So we learn from this prayer that joy is what Jesus wants in the life of every one of His followers. He wants us to have His joy, His delight, His enjoyment, and His gladness. One of the primary ways in which this transpires is by getting a revelation of what He said next: "They are not of the world, just a I am not of the world" (John 17:15).

Living an untroubled life in the midst of a troubled world begins with the revelation that we are not of this world. The phrase *not of the world* simply means our identity is not with this world. In other words, we don't identify with the world. If our identity is not with this world, then we are not subject to this world's boundaries. Whatever is controlling the rest of the world—whether it is chaos, lawlessness, or a bad economy—doesn't have to control us.

Jesus knew when He spoke to His disciples what was going to be happening in our current generation. He knows what we're going though now, and He knows what our future holds. He knew things were going to be bad in our times, yet He didn't pray we'd be taken out of the world but that we'd be protected from the evil one. And how, exactly, is God going to protect us? The Bible says, "For You, O LORD, will bless the righteous; with favor You will surround him as with a shield" (Psalm 5:12).

God has already placed a

> LIVING AN **UNTROUBLED LIFE** IN THE MIDST OF A TROUBLED WORLD BEGINS WITH THE REVELATION THAT WE ARE **NOT OF THIS WORLD**.

hedge of favor around us, around me and around you. It is the Spirit of favor that has been poured out upon our house. One commentary I read said God's favor is His defense and His protection for His people. The shield David is referring to in Psalm 5 describes a part of the armor used in his day. Unlike the little shields we see actors use in movies, the armor David refers to literally covered the entire body of a human being. It was large, it was broad, and it provided total protection. This is what David envisioned when he said God's favor surrounds the righteous as with a shield.

We became what David referred to as "the righteous" when Jesus was raised from the dead. And, at the same time, Jesus became our hedge of favor, in essence becoming the answer to His own prayer that we be protected from the evil one. Everywhere we go, we have something around us: the favor of God. It's a hedge that's been placed there by God to keep out the devil and what he's doing in the rest of the world.

The Hebrew word translated as *favor*, which we know can also be translated as the word grace, comes from two root words. The first word means "wall of separation." The illustration used to clarify this meaning was of an ancient Hebrew camp made up of many tents. When we think of a camp of tents, we envision a group of tents scattered all over an area. But that's not the way it was done in ancient times. The people formed camps by placing their tents in a circle—much like we see wagons forming a circle in a Western movie.

As Moses and Joshua led the Israelites through the wilderness, they didn't say, "Let's set up camp here for the night," and then just let everyone find a pretty place to pitch a tent. No, they formed a circle with their tents, creating a wall of separation between those in the camp and what was happening on the outside. Everything and everyone inside the wall was protected.

The favor of God was designed by God to form a wall of protection around His people, both individually and collectively, so that no matter what's happening to the rest of the world, it

> EVERYWHERE WE GO, WE HAVE SOMETHING AROUND US: **THE FAVOR OF GOD**.

doesn't affect us. We see this wall of protection illustrated as early as the book of Genesis with Abraham's son Isaac.

> There was a famine in the land, besides the first famine that was in the days of Abraham. And Isaac went to Abimelech king of the Philistines, in Gerar.
>
> Then the LORD appeared to him and said: "Do not go down to Egypt; live in the land of which I shall tell you. Dwell in this land, and I will be with you and bless you; for to you and your descendants I give all these lands, and I will perform the oath which I swore to Abraham your father."
>
> Then Isaac sowed in that land, and reaped in the same year a

hundredfold; and the LORD blessed him. The man began to prosper, and continued prospering until he became very prosperous; for he had possessions of flocks and possessions of herds and a great number of servants. So the Philistines envied him.

(Genesis 26:1–2, 12–14)

Although the world outside Isaac's wall of favor was in famine, Isaac was flourishing. His crops increased a hundredfold in the same year, to the point that the Philistines noticed and they envied him. The Philistines couldn't see that wall, but they knew it was there because here's what they said:

"We have certainly seen that the LORD is with you. So we said, 'Let there now be an oath between us, between you and us; and let us make a covenant with you, that you will do us no harm, since we have not touched you, and since we have done nothing to you but good and have sent you away in peace. You are now the blessed of the LORD.'"

(Genesis 26:28–29)

We can see in this illustration taken from the life of Isaac how God's favor created a "wall of separation" from what was going on in the rest of the world, just as the first root word for *favor* implies.

The other root word for *favor* means "to continue." In other words,

God's favor is a wall of separation that continues throughout an individual's life.

Because of the atoning work Jesus did at Calvary, we are saved by grace, through faith. And through the favor of our God, which He has bestowed upon His people, we now have this wall of separation that stands as a hedge of favor as long as we are living in this world. It's here for us when things are good and when they are bad. It's here for us when there's prosperity in the land and when there's recession in the land. And when everybody else is screaming, "There is no way," God's hedge of favor is here for us to make a way.

JOB'S HEDGE OF FAVOR

The Bible says Job was a man who feared God, a man who lived perfect and upright, a man who shunned evil. God had blessed Job in everything he set his hand to, making him the wealthiest man in the East.

The Amplified Bible describes Job as a man who "was blameless and upright, and one who [reverently] feared God and abstained from and shunned evil [because it was wrong] (Job 1:1). THE MESSAGE translation says Job was "totally devoted to God and hated evil with a passion."

We could say Job was a man after God's own heart, a man whom God could hold up like a trophy, which He might have been doing when He had this conversation with Satan.

"Have you considered My servant Job, that there is none like him on the earth, a blameless and upright man, one who fears God and shuns evil?"

So Satan answered the LORD and said, "Does Job fear God for nothing? Have You not made a hedge around him, around his household, and around all that he has on every side? You have blessed the work of his hands, and his possessions have increased in the land."

(Job 1:8–10)

THE MESSAGE translation says, "Why, no one ever had it so good! You pamper him like a pet, make sure nothing bad ever happens to him or his family or his possessions, bless everything he does—he can't lose!" (Job 1:10). Satan had obviously already launched attacks against Job and failed, which is how he must have known the hedge was there, around Job's life, his house, his substance, and his family.

If Job was already a good man, a man totally devoted to God who hated evil with a passion, then why did God put that wall around him to begin with? The Bible says, "He who earnestly seeks good finds favor" (Proverbs 11:27). The New International Version of this scripture says, "Whoever seeks good finds favor." The reason God put this wall around Job to start with was that he was a man who sought good. Proverbs clearly says that when God finds a person who seeks good and is determined to live for Him—to live morally right, to have morally good behavior and conduct, and to hate evil like He hates evil—then He will put His favor upon that individual. That hedge was a wall of God's favor, designed to separate Job and everything he had from whatever was happening outside that wall.

Job also understood that God's hedge was there, because he said, "Thou hast granted me life and favour, and thy visitation hast preserved my life" (Job 10:12 KJV). Job knew what he had on him, this hedge of favor that had given him the opportunities he needed to become a wealthy man. It was this hedge that Satan had been unable penetrate, and so he tried a different approach with God, saying, "But now, stretch out Your hand and touch all that he has, and he will surely curse You to Your face!"(Job 1:11).

This statement tells us Satan was trying to talk God into pulling down the hedge, since Satan didn't have the ability to do it himself. If he'd had the ability to do it, he wouldn't have asked God to do it. And God didn't do it.

You might be thinking, "What about all those attacks on Job's life? How did the hedge come down?" Well, if Satan couldn't pull down the hedge and God didn't do it, then that leaves only one person who had the ability to do it: Job.

THE HEDGE COMES DOWN

To understand what happened to Job's hedge of favor, let's look at God's answer to Satan, who had just challenged Him to stretch out His hand against Job: "And the LORD said to Satan, 'Behold, all that he has is in your power'" (Job 1:12). Now, this is an amazing statement. Apparently, the hedge was already down and Satan didn't know it. He mistakenly assumed the hedge was still there until God pointed out to him, "Job is in your power." But how did that come about?

Because we know that our faith activates God to move in our life and that fear opens the door for Satan to attack us, we can determine with reasonable assurance that Job opened the door to fear. And fear is what brought down that hedge. Here's what Job said after Satan's repeated attacks: "For the thing I greatly feared has come upon me, and what I dreaded has happened to me. I am not at ease, nor am I quiet" (Job 3:25–26). This statement tells us that, at some point in Job's life, he became fearful and stopped relying on his hedge of favor. What was he afraid of? I think it's pretty obvious: he was afraid of losing everything. He later said that he'd come into the world with nothing and he would leave with nothing.

After the hedge came down, Job became like the rest of the world. Whatever the world was going through, he was going through. Whatever attacks Satan launched successfully against the world, he launched successfully against Job.

The Bible tells us that when a hedge is removed, that which it surrounded will be trodden down by enemies (see Isaiah 5:5 AMP) and "whoso breaketh an hedge, a serpent shall bite him (Ecclesiastes 10:8 KJV). We know Satan is the serpent, so anytime we pull down our hedge of favor through fear, we are going to get bitten. Job brought down the hedge of favor around his house, and the first thing that happened was everything he possessed was trodden down. Next, he was bitten by the serpent, Satan.

When Satan first launched his attack against Job, resulting the loss of his children, his flocks, and his servants, the Bible says, "In all this Job did not sin nor charge God with wrong" (Job1:22). That's when Satan again went before God in an attempt to incite Him against Job:

And the LORD said to Satan, "From where do you come?

Satan answered the LORD and said, "From going to and fro on the earth, and from walking back and forth on it."

Then the LORD said to Satan, "Have you considered My servant Job, that there is none like him on the earth, a blameless and upright man, one who fears God and shuns evil? And still he holds fast to his integrity, although you incited Me against him, to destroy him without cause."

So Satan answered the LORD and said, "Skin for skin! Yes, all that a man has he will give for his life. But stretch out Your hand now, and touch his bone and his flesh, and he will surely curse You to Your face!"

And the LORD said to Satan, "Behold, he is in your hand, but spare his life."

So Satan went out from the presence of the LORD, and struck Job with painful boils from the sole of his foot to the crown of his head. And he took for himself a potsherd with which to scrape himself while he sat in the midst of the ashes.

Then his wife said to him, "Do you still hold fast to your integrity? Curse God and die!"

(Job 2:2–9)

Satan had apparently gotten to Job's wife. She urged Job to curse God, which is exactly what Satan had declared to God: "He will surely curse You!" Up until this point, Job had not sinned against God with his mouth, although we have evidence he had at some point already pulled down his hedge of favor through his fear. For the next seven days, as Job mourned in the silent presence of his friends, the venomous words spoken by his wife took root like seeds of bitterness in his soul. That's when he made this revealing declaration: "For the thing I greatly feared has come upon me, and what I dreaded has happened to me" (Job 3:25).

Job continued to suffer for a season, but he eventually came to the place where he understood many of his calamities were tied to what he had declared about fear. He said to the Lord, "Behold, I am vile; what shall I answer You? I lay my hand over my mouth. Once I have spoken, but I will not answer; yes, twice, but I will proceed no further" (Job 40:4–5). Job also said to God, "I have heard of You by the hearing of the ear, but now my eye sees You. Therefore I abhor myself, and repent in dust and ashes" (Job 42:5–6). And here's what happened following Job's prayer:

> Now the LORD blessed the latter days of Job more than his beginning; for he had fourteen thousand sheep, six thousand camels, one thousand yoke of oxen, and one thousand female donkeys. He also had seven sons and three daughters.
>
> After this Job lived one hundred and forty years, and saw his children and grandchildren for four generations. So Job died, old and full of days.
>
> (Job 42:12–13, 16–17)

The hedge of favor Job had pulled down through fear was resurrected through his faith in God. We, too, are surrounded by a hedge of God's favor. The Bible tells us "his favor lasts a lifetime!" (Psalm 30:5 NLT). It's on us for the rest of our lives. Satan can't pull it down, and God won't pull it down, so that only leaves us. And like Job, the way we pull it down is by opening the door to fear.

As people of faith, we must never let this happen.

CHAPTER 6
FAITH AND FEAR CANNOT EXIST

"Faster than a speeding bullet! More powerful than a locomotive! Able to leap tall buildings in a single bound. Look! Up in the sky. It's a bird. It's a plane. It's . . . Superman!"

Any kid who grew up in the 1950s knew these words by heart. They were the opening lines of each television episode of *The Adventures of Superman*, shot in black and white, and aired weekly.

There were certain indisputable facts all kids knew about Superman. He possessed powers and abilities far beyond those of mortal men, he could change the course of mighty rivers, and he could bend steel with his bare hands. Best of all, Superman fought the never-ending battle for truth, justice, and the American way.

But the man of steel had one weakness—*kryptonite,* a radioactive element from his home planet of Krypton. If he allowed himself to be exposed to the material, his strength was reduced to that of mortal beings.

Although kryptonite is a fictional element, in popular culture the word has come to mean "weakness" or "something to be avoided because of its harmful effects."

We could say that fear is to Christians what kryptonite is to Superman.

The command "Fear not" appears seventy-four times in the Bible, and "Be not afraid" appears twenty-nine times. Other derivatives are listed over three hundred times. Clearly, God's message in all of this is simple: "Do not fear!"

Fear is the opposite of faith. Just as faith activates God to move in a person's life, fear activates Satan to bring the very thing being feared into an individual's life. The best way to deal with any kind of fear is to confront it. The word *confront* means "to oppose in a direct and forceful way." That's why the first thing Jesus did in a critical situation was confront the fear.

When Jairus fell at the Lord's feet and begged Him to come to his home where his young daughter lay dying, Jesus followed immediately. Before they could get to the house, word came that the girl had died. Here is the Lord's response and the miracle that followed:

> But when Jesus heard it, He answered him, saying, "Do not be afraid; only believe, and she will be made well." When He came into the house, He permitted no one to go in except Peter, James, and John, and the father and mother of the girl. Now all wept and mourned for her; but He said, "Do not weep; she is not dead, but

sleeping." And they ridiculed Him, knowing that she was dead.

But He put them all outside, took her by the hand and called, saying, "Little girl, arise." Then her spirit returned, and she arose immediately.

(Luke 8:50–55)

The Bible says, "For God has not given us a spirit of fear, but of power and of love and of a sound mind" (2 Timothy 1:7). Fear is never to be tolerated in the life of a believer. It is a spirit that is to be cast out—just as Jesus did at the home of Jairus. Fear and faith cannot coexist.

So, if fear is not of God, then how does it come into a person's life? Fear comes to a person's life the same way faith comes—by hearing. The Bible says, "So then faith comes by hearing, and hearing by the word of God" (Romans 10:17). If we consistently hear the Word of God, we are going to grow in faith. But if we continually listen to negative opinions, negative philosophies, and our own negative thoughts—in essence creating an open door for fear to come—it most certainly will. That's why Jesus cautioned His followers to "take heed what you hear" (Mark 4:24).

Speaking of the world's wisdom, James described it as "earthly, sensual, devilish" (James 3:15). The NIV translation uses stronger language, calling it "earthly, unspiritual, demonic." Satan's purpose in exposing us to this worldly wisdom is to distract us from the promises of God and eventually cause us to fear what the world says will happen

IF WE **CONSISTENTLY** HEAR THE WORD OF GOD, WE ARE GOING TO **GROW** IN FAITH.

———

to us so that we bring down our hedge of favor. When we choose to listen to what the world says, we can expect fear to come. And if we listen long enough, we can expect to get exactly what Job got: great fear. Remember, Job said, "For the thing I greatly feared has come upon me, and what I dreaded has happened to me" (Job 3:25).

I can assure you, when you've allowed great fear to become developed inside you, then you're no longer looking to the favor of God for your protection. You don't confess God's favor. You don't think about it. You don't meditate on it. You're just consumed with all those bad things happening in the world, and if you fear them enough, then what you so greatly fear will come upon you. You're bringing down the hedge. That's why Proverbs 4:23 tells us, "Keep your heart with all diligence." The Amplified translation says, "Keep and guard your heart with all vigilance."

DON'T PLAY GAMES WITH FEAR

Jesus exposed Satan's agenda when He said, "The thief does not come except to steal, and to kill, and to destroy" (John 10:10). That's the devil's plan, and the number one tool he uses against us is fear. His number one objective in the earth today is to make God's people fearful. We can't play church and religious games with fear—there's too much at stake.

You simply cannot subject your spirit to the negative voices designed by Satan to distract you from the promises of God. Remember, his goal is to get you to pull down the hedge of favor. The Bible tells us to "keep a firm grip on the promises that keep us going" (Hebrews 10:23 THE MESSAGE). God has placed a hedge of favor around our lives, and He intends for it to remain there for our lifetime—despite what is going on with the rest of the world.

The apostle Paul said, "But know this, that in the last days perilous times will come" (2 Timothy 3:1). The Amplified Bible calls these "perilous times of great stress and trouble [hard to deal with and hard to bear]." Sounds pretty much like what we're facing in our world today, doesn't it?

Many people look to government for a solution. But the Republicans don't know how to fix things. The Democrats don't know how to fix things. The so-called experts are all saying, "The system is broken." Politicians don't know what to do—but we do!

We have a hedge of protection, a wall of separation, which separates us from what's happening out there—as long as we stay focused on the promises of God, maintain an attitude of faith, and don't bring that hedge down by opening the door to fear.

Long before I knew what the Word of God had to say about fear, I'd already learned how to confront my own fear in a direct and forceful way. When I was a little boy, there was a bully named Herbie who picked on me every day at school. One day I took some foreign coins to my class for show-and-tell, but Herbie took them from me.

GOD HAS PLACED A **HEDGE OF FAVOR** AROUND OUR LIVES, AND HE INTENDS FOR IT TO REMAIN THERE **FOR OUR LIFETIME**

That night when I told my dad what had happened, he said, "Son, I want you to get your coins back." And then he gave me a boxing lesson.

The next day at school I walked right up to Herbie, who was with a bunch of his friends, and delcared, "I want my coins back!"

Herbie just laughed at me, and then turned around to face his friends and proceeded to make fun of me. But a minute later when he turned back to face me, I punched him right in the nose. When he fell flat on his back, I jumped right on his chest and just worked him over. Sure enough, I got all my coins back. But the best part was when Herbie pleaded with me, "Little Jerry, please don't hit me no more!"

Herbie and I went all the way through high school together. Each year, Herbie got bigger and bigger—much bigger than me. But the funny thing was, every time Herbie saw me at school, he just moved to the other side of the hallway. What had happened? I'd simply confronted my fear.

Now, I don't want you to think I never again had to confront my fear. As long as we are in this world and we have an enemy who knows he can't get to us unless we pull down our own hedge of God's favor, we're going to have to confront fear. Even those who teach about faith and are competent with the Word of God have to deal with fear.

I remember John Osteen used to talk about his fear of flying. Just the thought of boarding an airplane would almost paralyze him, yet God had called him to go all over the world. He said the devil would tell him, "John, if you get on that airplane I'm going to kill you. It will crash, and you will die." But instead of giving up on the call God had placed upon his life, he confronted his fear by getting on that plane anyway. He confronted his fear, and he overcame it.

Fred Price has talked about his fear of being in the water. So what did he do? He learned to scuba dive. He faced his fear, confronted it, and overcame it.

God's hedge of favor is what distinguishes us from the rest of the world. It's what makes Satan say about us the same thing he said about Job, "He can't lose. No one has ever had it so good!" What if all of God's people lived like this in the world today? We'd see a major move of God in the earth that would leave those in the world wondering, "What is it with these people? They are not affected by what affects us." And we'd just say, "It's the favor of God upon our house. His favor surrounds us." You know what's going to happen next? They're going to say, "Show me your God—I want to know Him!" After all, that's God's purpose in pouring out His favor upon our house.

If you've made Jesus the Lord of your life, then the favor of God stands as a hedge around you. For some, the hedge may not be any higher than their feet right now because they've opened the door to fear. The good news is, the condition is reversible. All that's required is repentance for opening the door to fear, followed by a declaration of faith.

In my meetings, here's what I have people declare: "I declare that the Spirit of favor is upon my house. From this day forward, I expect the favor of God to operate in my life on a daily basis. I do not fear what the media says. I do not fear what the news says. I do not fear what the government says. I do not fear what unbelievers say, and I do not fear what unbelieving believers say. I believe the Word of God. His favor is upon my life. I'm surrounded by it, and I cannot lose!"

Standing in agreement with those who make this declaration of faith is just one of the ways I sow God's favor into the lives of others.

SOWING SEEDS OF FAVOR

I'll never forget the time my wife, my daughters, and I flew in our airplane to Houston, where I was scheduled to speak. On the final approach to the airport, we lost one of the engines. Fortunately, with that particular plane we were able to

> **GOD'S HEDGE** OF FAVOR IS WHAT **DISTINGUISHES** US FROM THE REST OF THE WORLD.

land safely using only the other engine, and we made it to the meeting without further incident.

We were scheduled to be someplace else the following morning, but there were no available commercial flights that could get us where we needed to be on time. I don't like to borrow anything from anyone, but at the time I had no other choice. I knew that because of my covenant relationship with Kenneth Copeland, I had access to his airplane. So I called him and asked if his plane and pilot were available to pick us up and take us to our next meeting. He said yes.

"Brother Copeland, I can't tell you how much I appreciate you," I said. "I am grateful to you for doing me this favor."

Then he told me something that went so deep into my heart that I'll never forget it. "That's what I'm here for," he said.

What a way to live—being mindful to be a blessing; to be gracious, to be kind, to sow seeds of favor when you're in the position to do so.

Listen to what the apostle Paul says about this kind of living: "Therefore, as we have opportunity, let us do good to all, especially to those who are of the household of faith" (Galatians 6:10). The Amplified Bible says to "be mindful to be a blessing." When a person does good or shows favor to someone else, the one doing good is actually sowing a seed. Seeds can come in the form of thoughts, words, deeds, and actions. Sowing is a law that was established in the book of Genesis.

God established the law of sowing and reaping when He said to

Adam, "See, I have given you every herb that yields seed which is on the face of all the earth, and every tree whose fruit yields seed; to you it shall be for food" (Genesis 1:29). Other translations say, "It shall be for provision." The point is, God was showing Adam how his life was to be sustained: he was to be a sower of seed. God went on to teach Adam that every seed produces after its own kind: you sow watermelon seeds and you get watermelons; you sow apple seeds and you get apples.

Even when God destroyed every living thing upon the earth and started over with Noah, the law of sowing and reaping remained intact. God said, "[Never] will I again destroy every living thing as I have done. While the earth remains, seedtime and harvest . . . shall not cease" (Genesis 8:21–22).

We see this law in both the Old Testament and the New Testament.

> SEEDS CAN COME IN THE FORM OF **THOUGHTS, WORDS, DEEDS, AND ACTIONS**.

It is a law God established, and its duration is until there is no more earth. As long as we are here on earth, the law of sowing and reaping remains in operation. It is either working for us or against us at all times, for the Bible says, "Do not be deceived, God is not mocked; for whatever a man sows, that will he also reap" (Galatians 6:7).

When we show favor to another person, we're actually sowing seed. And because every seed produces after its own kind, we know that if we sow favor, we will reap favor. A lot of people are believing for manifestations of the favor of God in their life, yet they seldom sow favor into the life of anyone else. In this world there are givers and takers; there are generous people and stingy people. There are those who are inclined to help people, and others who are always looking for help. I can't find anywhere in the Word where stingy people get blessed.

One time when Pastor Happy Caldwell and I were talking, he said, "Jerry, there are a lot of people, including some preachers, who do not understand reciprocity. I regularly sow seed into the lives of those who are preaching the gospel. But when I got to checking on some of the preachers who seemed to be asking for money all the time, I found out that many of them are not givers themselves."

When I heard this story, I remembered one minister in particular. Every time he invited me to speak at his church, he would ask me to personally sow into whatever project he had going on, and then he'd ask me to challenge his congregation to give as well. It seemed he wanted me to become a fundraiser for him, and I'm not a fundraiser.

> A LOT OF PEOPLE ARE **BELIEVING** FOR MANIFESTATIONS OF THE FAVOR OF GOD IN THEIR LIFE, YET THEY SELDOM **SOW FAVOR** INTO THE LIFE OF ANYONE ELSE.

So after I had this conversation with Pastor Happy, I returned to my office and went into the accounting department. I seldom go there, but this day I asked if they could show me the record of this particular minister and what he'd sown into our ministry. I'd been going to his church every year for more than ten years. And do you know how much he'd sown into our ministry? Zero. He'd never sown so much as a dime—not to our Africa outreaches, to a building fund, or anything else we'd done. Yet each time I saw him, he'd never fail to ask me to pray that he would walk in the same kind of favor I walk in.

According to Psalm 112, I was wasting my time praying for this man. He was neither gracious, nor did he show favor. He didn't disperse from what he had. He was a taker, not a giver. He was an opportunist looking to receive favor, not a man looking for an opportunity to sow favor.

Remember, God told Abraham, "I will bless you . . . and you shall be a blessing" (Genesis12:2). Regarding this scripture, I like this definition of blessing the Lord gave me years ago: "an instrument of God in which His divine favor flows into the life of another, preventing misfortune."

In the past two years alone, I've helped a number of ministers who have lost family members and haven't been in a position to pay for their loved-one's funeral. When I'd find out about their loss, I'd always ask the ministers if they were okay financially. If they said no, I'd ask what they needed. When they'd tell me, I would say, "That's what I'm here for," and then I'd sow a financial seed into their life.

Nothing can stop my sowing. There are only two times I sow: when I need to and when I don't. In other words, I'm sowing all the time. I believe what the Word of God says: I will reap what I sow. I sow the favor that is on my life, and in return I reap favor. I'm surrounded by it, and I cannot lose—regardless of the state of the economy.

I've learned that when the economy is bad, Satan will say to believers, "Times are getting tough, and they could get even worse. You can't give anymore." He's using fear to try to get you to hold on to everything you've got. He wants to instill the same fear in you that he instilled in Job: the fear of losing everything. Once you open the door to fear and drop your hedge of favor, it won't be long before the very thing you fear will come upon you. When times are bad is when you most need to be sowing. When the devil tells you that you can't sow, sow anyway. Sow in defiance of the enemy and in faith in the favor of God.

If you are dealing with a fear of financial failure or not having enough, confront that fear. Face it head on by sowing. Ask God to show you what is appropriate for you to sow, and where to sow it. Then when you sow, do it deliberately, in confident expectation that the favor of God upon you and your house will produce the

> THERE ARE ONLY **TWO TIMES** I SOW: WHEN I **NEED** TO AND WHEN I **DON'T**.

exact opportunity you need.

If you are at a place where you simply want to sow out of an attitude of gratitude for the favor of God upon your house, my prayer is that you will receive a harvest beyond what you can ask or think, so that you may be generous toward the work of the Lord.

Regardless of your present circumstances, I invite you to join me to confront and cast out fear in this spiritual declaration of independence:

"Satan, we do not fear you. We do not fear what you say. We are people of faith. We believe our God, and He is far greater than anything you are capable of doing. In the name Jesus, we take authority over the spirit of fear, and we cast it out. And we declare ourselves free in the name of Jesus!"

CHAPTER 7

A DIVINELY APPOINTED JUBILEE

In recent decades we've seen amazing changes in the way we live our daily lives. Technology has brought us cellular telephones, the Internet, and social media. On both the ground and in the air, we possess the ability to travel at speeds the Wright brothers could never have imagined when they made their historic, first-manned flight in an aircraft on December 17, 1903.

In this fast-paced and constant-contact culture we live in, our lives are oftentimes dictated by schedules and a seemingly never-ending list of appointments. We have business appointments, medical appointments, and lunch appointments, to name a few. Even our kids have schedules filled with weekly, extra-curricular appointments. Sometimes we end up getting so overbooked that we have to change appointments to accommodate our hectic schedules. It happens all the time.

Even though changing appointments may be a common occurrence for us, it is something never done on God's calendar. When God sets an appointment, it is established forever. We see an example of this in the feasts of the Lord, which were (and are) special prophetic occasions fixed by divine appointment.

> And the LORD spoke to Moses, saying, "Speak to the children of Israel, and say to them: 'The feasts of the LORD, which you shall proclaim to be holy convocations, these are My feasts.
> 'These are the feasts of the LORD, holy convocations which you shall proclaim at their appointed times.'"
>
> (Leviticus 23:1–2, 4)

The word *feast* used in this scripture is the Hebrew word *moed*, which means "an appointed or fixed time; an appointed place or meeting." On God's redemptive calendar for mankind, He established seven of these feasts, or moeds, one of which was the Day of Atonement. These feasts of the Lord were to be observed annually, but every fifty years there was to be a special observance on the Day of Atonement, the one day of the year when the high priest of Israel entered the Holy of Holies to offer a blood sacrifice for the sins of the people. This special, fifty-year observance was called the *Jubilee*.

> Then you shall cause the trumpet of the Jubilee to sound on the tenth day of the seventh month; on the Day of Atonement you shall make the trumpet to sound throughout all your land.

And you shall consecrate the fiftieth year, and proclaim liberty throughout all the land to all its inhabitants. It shall be a Jubilee for you; and each of you shall return to his possession, and each of you shall return to his family.

(Leviticus 25:9)

The blowing of the trumpets in the year of Jubilee signified restoration and freedom for the Israelites. Any land or property that had been sold as a result of poverty reverted without payment to the original owner or his lawful heirs. And every Israelite who had sold himself because of poverty to one of his countrymen, or a foreigner who had settled in the land, was to go free along with his children.

Unger's Bible Dictionary says, "For in this year every kind of oppression was to cease and every member of the covenant people find his Redeemer in the Lord, who brought him back to his possession and family."

As we read the description of the Jubilee in the book of Leviticus, we see that God's intention in instituting this appointed feast was to bless His people. The moment that horn was blown on the tenth day of the seventh month in the forty-ninth year, liberty was proclaimed throughout the land. Everything that had been taken was restored, and families that had been in captivity were set free. Again, this happened only once every fifty years. It was God's way of expressing His love and His desire to do good things for His people.

The Jubilee had been an integral part of Jewish life for centuries before Jesus was born. Everyone in His culture understood the significance of the Jubilee, including those gathered at the synagogue on one particular Sabbath day.

So He came to Nazareth, where He had been brought up. And as His custom was, He went into the synagogue on the Sabbath day, and stood up to read. And He was handed the book of the prophet Isaiah. And when He had opened the book, He found the place where it was written:

"The Spirit of the LORD is upon Me, because He has anointed Me to preach the gospel to the poor; He has sent Me to heal the brokenhearted, to proclaim liberty to the captives and recovery of sight to the blind, to set at liberty those who are oppressed; to proclaim the acceptable year of the LORD."

Then He closed the book, and gave it back to the attendant and sat down. And the eyes of all who were in the synagogue were fixed on Him. And He began to say to them, "Today this Scripture is fulfilled in your hearing."

(Luke 4:16–21)

Now remember, this was the synagogue Jesus had grown up in. Everybody there knew Him; He was the carpenter's boy. He'd been going there all His life, but on this particular day when He was handed the scroll, the Bible says He found the place where "it was written." This tells us that Jesus' action was deliberate; He went in there with something on His mind. Something was motivating Him to find a specific prophetic utterance in the book of Isaiah, which we know today as Isaiah 61.

What did Jesus mean when He said, "Today this Scripture is fulfilled in your hearing"? I like the way THE MESSAGE translation renders verse 21: "You've just heard Scripture make history." Jesus was saying, "You don't have to wait any longer for the man that Isaiah was prophesying about. He is here in your midst, and I am He! Today this Scripture is fulfilled in your ears."

God instituted the Jubilee as a type and shadow of redemption, of what Jesus would one day do for humanity at Calvary: Jesus Himself would become our Jubilee. For the next three and one-half years after Jesus read these words in the synagogue, He preached, He healed, He set the captives free, He restored sight to the blind, and He proclaimed the acceptable year of the Lord.

Interestingly, one of the definitions of the Hebrew word that is translated as acceptable is "favor." The Amplified Bible translates Luke 4:19 like this. "To proclaim the accepted and acceptable year of

> GOD INSTITUTED THE **JUBILEE** AS A TYPE AND SHADOW OF REDEMPTION, OF WHAT JESUS WOULD ONE DAY DO FOR HUMANITY AT **CALVARY**

the Lord [the day when salvation and the free favors of God profusely abound]." From the moment Jesus declared, "Today this Scripture is fulfilled in your ears," He was headed for Calvary. He knew that it was through Calvary alone that God's favor would be poured out profusely upon humanity.

Not only did Jesus fulfill Isaiah's prophecy when He became our Redeemer, our Jubilee, He also fulfilled Zechariah 12:10, which says, "And I will pour on the house of David and on the inhabitants of Jerusalem the Spirit of grace and supplication; then they will look on Me whom they pierced." The free favor of God was profusely poured out upon humanity, making all who would receive it members of the house of David. And for those who have received it, the favor of God is upon their house.

A TIME OF UNPRECEDENTED FAVOR

While Calvary marked the beginning of the time when salvation and the free favor of God were poured out upon humanity, the psalmist described a time of unprecedented favor yet to come.

But You, O LORD, shall endure forever, and the remembrance of Your name to all generations. You will arise and have mercy on Zion; for the time to favor her, yes, the set time, has come. For Your servants take pleasure in her stones, and show favor to her dust. So the nations shall fear the name of the LORD, and all the kings of the earth Your glory. For the LORD shall build up Zion; He shall appear in His glory. He shall regard the prayer of the destitute, and shall not despise their prayer. This will be written for the generation to come, that a people yet to be created may praise the LORD.

(Psalm 102:12–18)

While the term *Zion* used in the Old Testament generally refers to the fortress of the city of Jerusalem, it also has a prophetic significance. In the New Testament, Zion is symbolic of the Church. I believe the psalmist is seeing into the spirit realm when he says, in essence, "You will arise and have mercy or compassion on Your Church, for the time set to favor her has come."

So how do we know the psalmist wasn't talking about his own generation? His generation did experience the favor of God in ways. There were certainly manifestations of the favor of God throughout the Old Testament, but let's look again at verse 18: "This will be written for the generation to come, that a people ye to be created may praise the LORD."

The apostle Paul also spoke of a time that was to come, saying, "That in the ages to come He might show the exceeding riches of His grace in His kindness toward us in Christ Jesus" Ephesians 2:7).

We understand that Paul, like the psalmist, was seeing in the spirit realm. He was seeing something that was going to happen to a future generation. I've had people tell me this scripture is talking about when we get to heaven. Why would we need that kind of favor in heaven, when everything is perfect there? We need that kind of favor now, here on earth.

When Paul talks about God's grace and kindness toward us, that's you and me he's writing about. We know grace and favor are synonymous. Anytime we see the word grace, we can read it as *favor*: "that in the ages to come He might show the exceeding riches of His [favor] in His kindness toward us in Christ Jesus" (Ephesians 2:7).

The Amplified Bible gives us what I like to call the "unprecedented" version of this verse: "He did this that He might clearly demonstrate through the ages to come the immeasurable (limitless, surpassing) riches of His free grace (His unmerited favor) in [His] kindness and goodness of heart toward us in Christ Jesus."

The riches of God's favor are described as "immeasurable." I'd call that unprecedented. I'd also call "limitless" and "surpassing" unprecedented. We have entered into a time of unprecedented favor, in which God's favor will be immeasurable, limitless, and surpassing anything we've known before. A lot of people in both the Old Testament and the New Testament experienced God's favor, but not like what's headed our way.

The Lord said through the prophet Haggai, "The glory of this latter house shall be greater than the former" (Haggai 2:9). THE MESSAGE translation says, "A glorious beginning but an even more glorious finish." That's just the way God works; He never does less from generation to generation. He always does more. Psalm 115:14 declares, "May the LORD give you increase more and more, you and your children."

> A LOT OF PEOPLE IN BOTH THE OLD TESTAMENT AND THE NEW TESTAMENT EXPERIENCED GOD'S FAVOR, BUT **NOT** LIKE WHAT'S HEADED OUR WAY.

God has established on His redemptive calendar a time of unprecedented favor for His Church, the Body of Christ. That set time has now come, and neither the government nor a bad economy can prevent God from carrying out His purpose for our generation. In Ephesians 3:20, Paul says, "[God] is able to do exceedingly abundantly above all that we ask or think." The Amplified translation says, "[He] is able to [carry out His purpose and] do superabundantly, far over and above what we [dare] ask or think [infinitely beyond our highest prayers, desire, thoughts, hopes, or dreams]." And THE MESSAGE says, "[God can do] far more than you could ever imagine or guess or request in your wildest dreams!"

What I hear Paul telling us is simply this: Don't limit God! Stop thinking small; become a big thinker, a big dreamer, a big believer. God is in the business of fulfilling His purpose. Why? Because He's a covenant-keeping God, because He loves us. Every thought He has about you is for the purpose of making your life better. His plans for you are filled with His goodness.

God spoke these words through Jeremiah: "And My people shall be satisfied with My goodness" (Jeremiah 31:14). The 1828 edition of *Webster's Dictionary* defines *goodness* as "acts of kindness and favor." What is God telling us? That He is going to pour out His favor upon us until we are satisfied. I am grateful for what I've seen and what I've experienced, but God says there is more. And if there's more, that means I'm not satisfied yet. There's more for this generation to experience.

I looked up the word *satisfied* and found out it means "to fully supply until we are content." I believe this is the kind of contentment David described when he said, "My cup runs over" (Psalm 23:5). Our God is a cup-running-over God; He's a God who is more than enough. The favor already being poured out profusely upon us is beyond anything humankind has experienced before. We've entered a time of unprecedented favor, and with that favor comes a holy shaking.

A HOLY SHAKING

We just read the words of the prophet Haggai describing the time in which we live as one where the glory of the latter house will be greater than the glory of the former. But immediately preceding this statement, he makes an interesting proclamation. Let's read the entire portion of scripture in context:

"For thus says the LORD of hosts: 'Once more (it is a little while) I will shake heaven and earth, the sea and dry land; and I will

shake all nations, and they shall come to the Desire of All Nations, and I will fill this temple with glory,' says the LORD of
hosts. 'The silver is Mine, and the gold is Mine,' says the LORD
of hosts. 'The glory of this latter temple shall be greater than the
former,' says the LORD of hosts. 'And in this place I will give
peace,' says the LORD of hosts."

(Haggai 2:6–9)

God is saying that in a little while He is going to shake some things
up. I love God's sense of humor. When He says, "A little while," that
could mean thousands of years to Him. Then a thousand years could
pass, and He calls it, "Suddenly." What God is saying in this passage
is this: "I'm going to fill this house with My glory. And by the way, the
gold and the silver is Mine, and I'm going to shake it loose."

There is a wealth transfer coming, and Satan is not going to be
able to hold on to what he's been holding back from the Body of
Christ. There are some houses that belong to God's people. There are
some businesses that belong to God's people. There are finances that
belong to God's people, and there is wealth that belongs to God's people. We have entered into a time of unprecedented favor, and God is
going to shake loose the harvest that belongs to you and to me. In the
book of James we see an indictment against the rich oppressor.

Come now, you rich, weep and howl for your miseries that are
coming upon you! Your riches are corrupted, and your garments

> THERE IS A **WEALTH TRANSFER** COMING, AND SATAN IS NOT GOING TO BE ABLE TO HOLD ON TO WHAT HE'S BEEN HOLDING BACK FROM THE **BODY OF CHRIST**.
>
> ═══

are moth-eaten. Your gold and silver are corroded, and their corrosion will be a witness against you and will eat your flesh like fire. You have heaped up treasure in the last days. Indeed the wages of the laborers who mowed your fields, which you kept back by fraud, cry out; and the cries of the reapers have reached the ears of the Lord.

(James 5:1–3)

Although they do not realize it, the ungodly rich have heaped wealth only to be given to the Body of Christ in these last days. Proverbs 13:22 says, "The wealth of the sinner is laid up for the just." God fully intends to place this wealth into the hands of those who have a passion for souls so that they may use the wealth to evangelize the world. Let's keep reading:

> Indeed the wages of the laborers who mowed your fields, which you kept back by fraud, cry out; and the cries of the reapers have reached the ears of the Lord of Sabaoth.
>
> (James 5:4)

Notice first, the wages belonging to the laborers have been kept back by fraud. Secondly, the cries of those who've been defrauded have entered the ears of the Lord of Sabaoth, which means "the Lord of hosts." If we look back to Haggai 2, we see it was the Lord of hosts who was speaking through the prophet. As we study these scriptures from both the Old Testament and New Testament, we have a clear understanding of what God is saying: The wages and finances that make up the harvest, which rightfully belongs to the Body of Christ, are crying out. And at the same time, the Body of Christ, to whom the harvest belongs, is also crying out. God hears both of these cries.

Your harvest is crying out for you every day, saying, "I don't belong to the ungodly, to the sinful—I belong to you!" If we will cry out for the harvest, just as the harvest is crying out for us, the Lord of hosts will hear us. That harvest is crying out to come into the hands of those to whom it rightfully belongs. Because Jesus is our Jubilee, all that rightfully belongs to us as the Body of Christ is being restored.

The psalmist wrote, "Thy people shall be willing in the day of thy power" (Psalm 110:3 KJV). When God's people start seeing the outpouring of the unprecedented favor of God, the goodness of God, the power of God, and they see the shaking going on, they will be willing to do whatever they need to do to show God that He holds first place in their lives. They will say, "Everything I have, I owe to you, and I'm willing to give it all to you." And it was Jesus—our Jubilee—who said, "Assuredly, I say to you, there is no one who has left house or

BECAUSE JESUS IS OUR **JUBILEE**, ALL THAT RIGHTFULLY BELONGS TO US AS THE BODY OF CHRIST IS **BEING RESTORED**.

═══

brothers or sisters or father or mother or wife or children or lands, for My sake and the gospel's, who shall not receive a hundredfold now in this time—houses and brothers and sisters and mothers and children and lands" (Mark 10:29–30).

I like the way THE MESSAGE sums it up: "No one's ever seen or heard anything like this, never so much as imagined anything quite like it—what God has arranged for those who love him" (1 Corinthians 2:9).

CHAPTER 8

NEVER GIVE UP

I am always blessed when I have the opportunity to pray for people following a service. One particular evening, a man who'd been waiting in line to see me for quite a while approached me with an unusual prayer request.

"Brother Jerry, would you please pray for me?"

"Sure," I said. "What would you like me to pray?"

"That I'll never have another test or trial in my life," he told me. Then he closed his eyes and bowed his head.

I laid my hands on him and prayed, "Lord, let him die!"

"What!" he declared, as his head snapped up and his eyes popped open.
"What are you saying?"

"Didn't you just say you didn't ever want to have another challenge?"

"Yes, but "

"Sir, the only way I know that this can happen is if you die and go to heaven," I told him.

"But I don't want to die," he said.

"Then you'd better learn how to face your trials and challenges and overcome them with the Word of God. I suggest you start by declaring God's favor over your house."

"Thanks, Brother Jerry. That's just what I'm going to do."

So I laid my hands on him again and said, "Lord, let him live and see the Spirit of favor upon his house."

As long as we are alive on this planet, we are going to have adversity; none of us are exempt. But the thing that makes us as believers different from the world is the blessing and the favor of God upon our houses. The world doesn't know where to turn in adversity and, sadly, neither do some Christians. But, thank God, even in the midst of the worst challenge we could ever face in our lives, we can be confident that we have something resting upon us that is far greater than any challenge: it's the blessing and the favor of God.

Of course, the devil will say, "Wait a minute. If you have this empowerment on you to prosper and succeed, then why are you going through this trial? Apparently what God said is not so." My friend, you can go through the Bible and find that everywhere it talks about the blessing of God being on a certain individual, that same person went

> THE THING THAT MAKES US AS BELIEVERS **DIFFERENT** FROM THE WORLD IS THE **BLESSING** AND THE **FAVOR** OF GOD UPON OUR HOUSES.

through some challenges. Take, for instance, the life of Joseph.

Most of us are familiar with the story of Joseph, the youngest son of Jacob and a direct descendant of Abraham. Because Joseph was the son of Jacob's old age, Jacob expressed his special love for the boy by making him a distinctive tunic.

Not long afterward, God visited Joseph and gave him a dream. When he told his brothers he had seen them bowing down to him in the dream, it upset them greatly—to the point of extreme hatred—and they began putting together a plot to get rid of him. They threw him into a pit where they kept him until they sold him to a caravan of Ismaelites who took him captive into Egypt. The brothers then took his garment, dipped it in the blood of a goat, and showed it to their father, causing him to believe Joseph had been devoured by a wild beast. As Jacob mourned the loss of his beloved son, Joseph was being sold as a slave to a man named Potiphar, one of Pharaoh's officers.

A direct descendant of Abraham, Joseph most certainly had the blessing of God on his life—and yet he was sold into slavery. Perhaps the lesson we must learn here is that the blessing will not exempt us from challenges; nevertheless, if we know how to appropriate and walk in it, we can overcome any adversity we may be facing just as Joseph did.

The Bible says, "*The LORD was with* Joseph, and he was a successful man; and he was in the house of his master the Egyptian. And his master saw that *the LORD was with* him and the LORD made all he did to prosper" (Genesis 39:2–4 italics mine). Anytime we see the phrase *the LORD was with*, we understand favor and the blessing are there as well.

Let's take a quick look at two of Joseph's anscestors whom God was also with.

Two generations prior to Joseph's birth, there had been a famine in the land. During that time many people journeyed to Egypt to find food, but God appeared to Joseph's grandfather, Isaac, saying, "Dwell in this land, and I *will be with* you and bless you" (Genesis 26:3 italics mine). That is exactly what God did for Isaac, just as he had done for Isaac's father, Abraham.

When the time had come for Abraham and his nephew Lot to separate their vast herds and wealth, Abraham had given Lot first choice of which land to dwell in. Lot had chosen the land that appeared to be the most favorable, a place where it would be easy to flourish and prosper, leaving Abraham with the desert. But Abraham had known the blessing of God and the favor of God was upon him, and in a little while God had made the desert to bloom and Abraham had flourished. The land Lot had chosen turned out to be Sodom and Gomorah.

WHEN WE FLOURISH, OTHERS SEE GOD

God's blessing and favor upon someone will cause them to flourish, no matter where they are. They will flourish in places where nobody else is flourishing. They will flourish if they are in a jail, and they will flourish if they are in a third-world country.

When I first started going to the continent of Africa some thirty-five years ago, I went to the bush. It was a place where people lived in mud huts with no running water and no electricity. They didn't have nice houses or any means of transportation or jobs. The Lord said to me, "I didn't send you here just to evangelize. I sent you to disciple. These people need to be taught my Word; they need to be grounded in my Word."

I immediately cancelled the evangelistic meetings I had scheduled, and gathered the eighty local pastors and ministers who had been part of the crusade. I spent eight services with them, teaching them the basics of redemptive truth. I knew if eighty local pastors could get grounded in the revelation of God's blessing and favor, they could change the nation. Not surprisingly, my message was met with resistance. Not from the local pastors, but from the American missionaries.

"You can't teach these people about blessing and prosperity," the missionaries insisted. "These people are poor! Besides, prosperity is an American message."

Seriously? That makes about as much sense as saying, "You can't teach these people about salvation—they're lost." Well, I was determined to prove this Bible message was more than an American message, especially since not one single American participated in writing the Bible. I was determined to prove that God's Word and the empowerment of His blessing and favor will create the opportunity for anyone to prosper—even people living in a third-world country where nobody had been prospering.

We started with a group of eighty people who were hungry for the redemptive truth of God. We went there regularly to teach them the Word and provide the resources they needed to teach their people. That group of eighty pastors has since established more than fifty churches. I've seen that many of the same people who once lived in mud huts are now living in houses. People who used to walk everywhere they went now have bicycles or cars. Many who had no way to earn an income now own businesses. This is what the blessing will do. If it will cause people in the African bush to flourish, it will do the same anywhere.

> IF EIGHTY LOCAL PASTORS COULD GET GROUNDED IN THE **REVELATION** OF GOD'S BLESSING AND FAVOR, THEY COULD **CHANGE THE NATION**.

But God doesn't want us to flourish for the sole reason of making our lives better; He wants others to see the effect of His blessing and favor so that they'll be attracted to Him. He wants us to prosper and succeed to get the attention of a world that has a misconception about God. When we prosper and succeed because the blessing of God is upon our lives, it makes us attractive to a world that doesn't know

Him. This is a biblical principal, clearly illustrated in the life of Joseph when he was a slave in the house of Potiphar.

The LORD was with Joseph, and he was a successful man; and he was in the house of his master the Egyptian. And his master saw that the LORD was with him and that the LORD made all he did to prosper in his hand. So Joseph found favor in his sight, and served him. Then he made him overseer of his house, and all that he had put under his authority. So it was, from the time that he had made him overseer of his house and all that he had, that the LORD blessed the Egyptian's house for Joseph's sake; and the blessing of the LORD was on all that he had in the house and in the field."

(Genesis 39:2–5)

The blessing of God provided Joseph with the empowerment to prosper, but favor produced the opportunity for his promotion to overseer. Oftentimes, when we are going through a negative

> WHEN WE **PROSPER AND SUCCEED** BECAUSE THE BLESSING OF GOD IS UPON OUR LIVES, IT MAKES US **ATTRACTIVE** TO A WORLD THAT DOESN'T KNOW HIM.

set of circumstances, we believe there is no possibility of something good turning out of it. But this is not true. In fact, it was Joseph who later said that what his brothers had meant for bad, God had turned around for something good. God can always turn what Satan means for bad into something good.

One of my favorite Bible verses comes from Paul's first letter to the church at Corinth as he was talking about Jesus' crucifixion. Paul said, "Had they known, they would not have crucified the Lord of glory" (1 Corinthians 2:8). Had Satan known what was going to happen three days later, he would never have incited his followers to take Jesus to the cross. Every time the devil comes against me, I like to say, "Okay, here you go again. You ought to know by now that I don't quit, I don't give up. I'm going to see this thing through, and I'm telling you right now, I'm coming out on the other side with a major victory. Had you known, you wouldn't have messed with me."

God has the ability to turn what appears to be an impossibly bad situation into something unimaginably good.

HAD SATAN **KNOWN** WHAT WAS GOING TO HAPPEN THREE DAYS LATER, HE WOULD **NEVER** HAVE INCITED HIS FOLLOWERS TO TAKE JESUS TO THE CROSS.

WE WALK BY FAITH

If you are facing adversity and challenges right now and it doesn't look as though the blessing and favor are working in your life, remember this: "we walk by faith, not by sight" (2 Corinthians 5:7). It may not look like blessing and favor are working, but they are working. It's just a matter of time before you see the manifestation.

Don't ever give up on the blessing, and don't ever give up on favor. The battle is not over until God has the final say. One of the greatest lessons we can learn while waiting for the blessing and favor to manifest is to avoid complaining, murmuring, and becoming distracted by the fact that it doesn't look like anything is happening. The truth is, something is happening; we just can't see it with our natural eyes. When we stay focused on God and maintain a right attitude through our trials, we are headed for a major victory. Attitude is everything.

Sadly, some Christians are worse than worldly people where their attitude is concerned. There are some downright ungodly people I would rather be around than some Christians. The ungodly don't know any better; but there's no excuse when Christians display a wrong attitude—or "stinkin' thinkin'," as I like to call it. I don't like to be around Christians who behave like that. I'll pray for them, and I'll preach to them, but it's not likely they'll become my personal friends.

> WHEN WE STAY **FOCUSED** ON GOD AND MAINTAIN A RIGHT ATTITUDE THROUGH OUR TRIALS, WE ARE HEADED FOR A MAJOR **VICTORY**.

Perhaps you have a worldly boss who is the meanest, most stinkin'-thinkin' person you've ever met in your life. If you maintain a right attitude while you believe for the blessing to manifest in that environment, your boss will soon recognize that you are excelling in your work. And maybe, just maybe, that mean boss who needs to get saved will become very fond of you. When this happens, God has promotion in store for you. That's what happened to Joseph.

Joseph maintained a right attitude through the trial of is slavery. He believed God had given him his dream, and he believed in the blessing and favor of God upon his life. He did not let his negative circumstances distract him. I like the way THE MESSAGE describes the outcome of Joseph's behavior.

> As it turned out, GOD was with Joseph and things went very well with him. He ended up living in the home of his Egyptian master. His master recognized that GOD was with him, saw that GOD was working for good in everything he did. He became very fond of Joseph and made him his personal aide. He put him in charge of all his personal affairs, turning everything over to him. From that moment on, GOD blessed the home of the Egyptian—all because of Joseph. The blessing of GOD spread over everything he owned, at home and in the fields, and all Potiphar had to concern himself with was eating three meals a day.
>
> (Genesis 39:2–6 THE MESSAGE)

In the midst of what appeared to be a negative situation in Joseph's life, God's blessing and favor were working. The blessing was empowering Joseph to prosper; favor was producing the opportunity for promotion. Potiphar made Joseph, a slave, his personal aide.

God's favor is continually producing opportunities for you to rise above your situation. You cannot allow yourself to be distracted by the negative things happening in your life. Stay focused on God and His blessing and favor, and keep trusting in the dream He has given you. That dream is a promise that will come to pass, and even the devil himself is not able to stop it.

Things were definitely looking up for Joseph. He was still not living his dream, but things had become more comfortable on his journey. No longer treated like a slave, Joseph had charge over everything Potiphar owned because of God's manifested blessing and favor. And this blessing and favor did not go unnoticed by others, including Potiphar's wife.

And it came to pass after these things that his master's wife cast longing eyes on Joseph, and she said, "Lie with me."

But he refused and said to his master's wife, "Look, my master does not know what is with me in the house, and he has committed all that he has to my hand. There is no one greater in this house than I, nor has he kept back anything from me but you, because you are his wife. How then can I do this great wickedness, and sin against God?"

So it was, as she spoke to Joseph day by day, that he did not heed her, to lie with her or to be with her.

But it happened about this time, when Joseph went into the house to do his work, and none of the men of the house was inside, that she caught him by his garment, saying, "Lie with me." But he left his garment in her hand, and fled and ran outside.

So she kept his garment with her until his master came home. Then she spoke to him with words like these, saying, "The Hebrew servant whom you brought to us came in to me to mock me; so it happened, as I lifted my voice and cried out, that he left his garment with me and fled outside."

So it was, when his master heard the words which his wife spoke to him, saying, "Your servant did to me after this manner," that his anger was aroused. Then Joseph's master took him and put him into the prison, a place where the king's prisoners were confined. And he was there in the prison.

(Genesis 39:7–12, 16–20)

Some may wonder, "If the blessing is the empowerment to prosper and favor produces opportunity, then why was Joseph thrown into prison?" Blessing and favor don't exempt us from adversity, but they do exempt us from being defeated.

Joseph had clearly experienced a setback. He was once again in the pit, and this time there seemed to be no way out, no way for the dream God had given him years earlier ever to come to pass. Even in prison, Joseph never changed his attitude; he never became critical of God. He didn't murmur or complain, although it looked like God had brought him this far and let him down. But the story wasn't over. In what was probably the darkest period of time Joseph had yet experienced, God's favor was at work producing an opportunity.

But the LORD was with Joseph and showed him mercy, and He gave him favor in the sight of the keeper of the prison. And the keeper of the prison committed to Joseph's hand all the prisoners who were in the prison; whatever they did there, it was his doing. The keeper of the prison did not look into anything that was under Joseph's authority, because the LORD was with him; and whatever he did, the LORD made it prosper.

> BLESSING AND FAVOR DON'T **EXEMPT** US FROM ADVERSITY, BUT THEY DO EXEMPT US FROM BEING **DEFEATED**.

(Genesis 39:21–23)

Here was Joseph, sitting in prison because of a false accusation, and he becomes the assistant to the keeper of the prison. He was in prison, but he wasn't treated like a prisoner. Because the Lord was with Joseph, so were His blessing and favor. This tells us that no matter what anyone could do to Joseph, God's blessing and favor would always cause him to rise above his circumstances.

We should never allow the thought that "setbacks are final" become part of our mindset. Setbacks are not final! They can become our steppingstones to a major victory—if we keep a right attitude.

While Joseph was in prison, Pharaoh had two dreams that troubled him. Though he called together his magicians and wise men, none could interpret the meaning of the dreams. That's when one of his servants who had done a stint in prison under Joseph's charge told Pharaoh about the young Hebrew man who could interpret dreams.

> SETBACKS ARE NOT FINAL! THEY CAN **BECOME** OUR STEPPINGSTONES TO A MAJOR **VICTORY**—IF WE KEEP A RIGHT ATTITUDE.

Pharaoh summoned Joseph from the prison and told him the two dreams. Joseph explained that God had given him the dreams to show Pharaoh what He was about to do in the land. Joseph said, "And the dream was repeated to Pharaoh twice because the thing is established by God, and God will shortly bring it to pass" (Genesis 41:32).

Favor had again created an opportunity for Joseph. Here's what happened next:

Then Pharaoh said to Joseph, "Inasmuch as God has shown you all this, there is no one as discerning and wise as you. You shall be over my house, and all my people shall be ruled according to your word; only in regard to the throne will I be greater than you." And Pharaoh said to Joseph, "See, I have set you over all the land of Egypt."

(Genesis 41:39–41)

Bible scholars agree that the period of time between Joseph being sold by his brothers to his rise to governor of Egypt was approximately seventeen years. I know some Christians who've said, "Oh, Brother Jerry, I've been going through this trial for a whole month. When is it going to stop?" How about you? Like Joseph, could you maintain your focus on what God promised you even if it took years to come to pass? Like Paul, could you declare in the midst of the worst adversity you'd ever experienced, "None of these things move me" (Acts 20:24)? That's the way Joseph viewed his adversity, which eventually paid off in a big way.

Joseph prospered in his position. He married and became the father of two sons: *Manasseh*, which means "God has made me forget all my toil and all my father's house," and *Ephraim*, meaning "God has caused me to be fruitful in the land of my affliction." Later, when a famine had come over all the face of the earth, Joseph opened the storehouses of grain and sold it to those who had journeyed to Egypt for food. Unbeknownst to Joseph, his father, Jacob, who thought him long dead, had sent his brothers to buy grain.

So Joseph's ten brothers went down to buy grain in Egypt.

Now Joseph was governor over the land; and it was he who sold to all the people of the land. And Joseph's brothers came and bowed down before him with their faces to the earth.

Joseph saw his brothers and recognized them, but he acted as a stranger to them and spoke roughly to them. Then he said to them, "Where do you come from?"

And they said, "From the land of Canaan to buy food."

So Joseph recognized his brothers, but they did not recognize him. Then Joseph remembered the dreams which he had dreamed about them.

(Genesis 42:3, 6–9)

We can only imagine what Joseph might have been thinking and feeling at that moment. Here before him were his own brothers, bowing down to him—just as he had seen in his dream. In the years since he had seen his family, he'd been sold as a slave, falsely accused of an act he did not commit, and imprisoned. Yet the blessing of God had empowered him to prosper in times of great trial and adversity, and the favor of God had created unimaginable opportunities for him to rise above his circumstances.

So much time had passed, Joseph's brothers didn't even recognize him. He'd only been a boy of seventeen when they had sold him; now he was a grown man of great stature. He had the power to retaliate against them for what they had done to him, yet he didn't. Throughout his years of adversity, Joseph had maintained a right attitude; it was now part of his character. Instead of executing vengeance, Joseph chose to extend the blessing and favor that were upon his house to his brothers.

Then Joseph said to his brothers, "I am Joseph; does my father still live?" But his brothers could not answer him, for they were dismayed in his presence. And Joseph said to his brothers, "Please come near to me." So they came near. Then he said: "I am Joseph your brother, whom you sold into Egypt. But now, do not therefore be grieved or angry with yourselves because you sold me here; for God sent me before you to preserve life. For these two years the famine has been in the land, and there are still five years in which there will be neither plowing nor harvesting. And God sent me before you to preserve a posterity for you in the earth, and to save your lives by a great deliverance. So now it was not you who sent me here, but God; and He has made me a father to Pharaoh, and lord of all his house, and a ruler throughout all the land of Egypt.

"Hurry and go up to my father, and say to him, 'Thus says your son Joseph: "God has made me lord of all Egypt; come down to me, do not tarry. You shall dwell in the land of Goshen, and you shall be near to me, you and your children, your children's children, your flocks and your herds, and all that you have."

(Genesis 45:3–9)

Not only was Joseph reconciled to the dream he had carried for years, seeing it fulfilled before his very eyes, but he also was reconciled with his family. The impossible became possible. That's what the favor of God does in our lives.

Perhaps you've had a dream God put in your heart years ago that now seems virtually impossible to be fulfilled. Or maybe you've faced so much adversity and loss that you can't even envision your life being different than it is now. I would remind you that Jesus said, "In the world you will have tribulation; but be of good cheer, I have overcome the world" (John 16:33).

On the other hand, you may say, "But, Brother Jerry, I already have all I ever dreamed of in this life. I am blessed, and the favor of God has already prospered me." If this is you, I would remind you that God "is able to do exceedingly abundantly above all that we ask or think, according to the power that works in us" (Ephesians 3:20).

Regardless of your present circumstances, the Spirit of favor is upon your house. It is a power that is working in concert with the Spirit of God within you to bring you into the fullness of the blessing that God has already provided for you. Don't ever give up on God. Don't ever give up on His blessing. Don't stop believing in the favor of God, and don't think because you have enough that God doesn't have more for you.

After all, if you've received Jesus Christ as your Savior and Lord, then *the Spirit of favor is on your house!*

Dr. Jerry Savelle was an average, blue-collar man who was struggling and needed God's help. While he considered himself a "nobody," when he became a believer God told him not to worry about it because He was a master at making champions out of nobodies. God has since taken Dr. Savelle from being a constant quitter to a man who knows how to stand on the Word of God until victory is experienced. Because of the life-changing combination of God's faithfulness and Dr. Savelle's "no quit" attitude, his life is totally different today.

Since 1969, Dr. Savelle has been traveling the world teaching people how to win in life. Dr. Savelle has ministered in more than three thousand churches in twenty-six nations, and has overseas offices in the United Kingdom, Australia, Canada, and Tanzania, Africa.

God has used Dr. Savelle to impact people who are burned out on religion and who have backslidden in their walk with God, as well as Christians who have a need to hear the Word of God presented in terms applicable to their lives, dreams, and destinies. He is the host of the Jerry Savelle Ministries television broadcast which airs in two hundred countries worldwide.

Dr. Savelle is the author of more than seventy books, including his bestsellers, *If Satan Can't Steal Your Joy, He Can't Keep Your Goods, Called to Battle, Destined To Win,* and *Prayer of Petition.* He and his wife, Carolyn, also serve as founding Pastors of Heritage of Faith Christian Center in Crowley, Texas.

FURTHER RESOURCES FROM JERRY SAVELLE

JERRYSAVELLE.ORG

-Digital Magazine App
-On-Demand TV Programs
-Product Specials
-Video/Audio Downloads
-Tour Dates
-And Much More...